30169

AMAZING DISCOVERIES

within the
BOOK
of
BOOKS

D1554619

Ralph Woodrow Evangelistic Association, Inc.

©Copyright 1979
Library of Congress Catalog Card Number: 79-55970
ISBN: 0-916938-04-2

San Jose Bible College Library
790 S. 12th St., P.O. Box 1090
San Jose, California 95108

SINGLE COPIES:
$3.00
(Quantity prices upon request)

Additional copies of this book may be obtained
through your local bookstore, or by writing to:

RALPH WOODROW
POST OFFICE BOX 124
RIVERSIDE, CALIFORNIA 92502

CONTENTS

INTRODUCTION

Though the Bible is a well-known book, nevertheless there remain *many* things within its pages that have been neglected, misunderstood, or overlooked. It is about these things that this book has been written. We are reminded of Apollos. Though he was a preacher, "an eloquent man, and mighty in the scriptures", yet he received much more truth when Aquila and Priscilla "expounded unto him the way of God *more perfectly*" (Acts 18:24-28). It is our hope that this book, by the grace of God, can serve in just that capacity.

In the pages which follow, you will be able to read in a comparatively short time things that I have come to know only through *years* of study.

We will have occasion to quote some very old books such as *Jasher, Philo,* and *Josephus.* The background information which these provide is helpful in our study of the Bible, but—and we would emphasize this—we certainly do not put these books on a level with the Bible itself.

There are over one thousand (1,022) questions in the New Testament and over two thousand (2,272) questions in the Old Testament of the Bible. Some of the most outstanding passages in the Bible were given in answer to *questions*—passages such as the message to Nicodemus about being born again (John 3), Christ's prophecy on the Mount of Olives (Matthew 24), Peter's message on the day of Pentecost (Acts 2) and Paul's teaching on marriage (1 Corinthians 7).

Some of the questions we will discuss are these: Where did Cain get his wife? Did it rain on the earth before the time of the flood? Did it take 120 years to build the Ark? Did Noah put a curse on Ham? What woman's age is mentioned in the Bible and why? Who was the Ethiopian wife of Moses? Why did Balaam want the children of Israel to be involved in ritual prostitution? Did the Israelites wear the same clothing for forty years—clothing that would not wear out? Did they eat only manna for forty years? Were they all healed when they came out of Egypt? Is physical healing in the atonement?

When Jonah refused to go to Nineveh, why did he choose

Tarshish instead? Did Elijah go to heaven? If so, why did Jesus say that no man had ascended up to heaven? After killing a thousand Philistines, did Samson drink water out of a jawbone? Did ravens feed the prophet Elijah—or was it Arabians? Did Delilah cut off Samson's hair? Did Absalom get his hair caught in the limb of a tree? What did Jeremiah mean when he spoke of a "speckled bird"? Are expressions such as "immortal soul", "trinity", "rapture", and "virgin birth" found in the Bible? Is the King James Version in use today the same as that of 1611?

What is the meaning of the number 153—the number of fish that Peter caught? Was Judas the son of Peter? Did Jesus fall beneath his cross? Or did he even carry the cross to Calvary? Was the crucifixion on a hill? The tomb in which Jesus was buried was in a garden—what kind of garden was it? Did Jesus ascend to heaven from the Mount of Olives? Were the disciples in the "upper room" on the day of Pentecost? Were there only 120 on that occasion?

Along with the serious doctrinal studies within these pages, I made a decision to include a bit of humor here and there. Some sanctimonious individuals may not like this, but as I heard a preacher say years ago, "Some people have a face so long they could suck marbles out of a gopher hole." Long faces are O.K. on mules up in Missouri, but no good on Christians in California (or anywhere else)! After all, "a merry heart doeth *good*" and "maketh a *cheerful* countenance" (Proverbs 17:22; 15:13).

Some of the material is of a technical nature which will probably be of interest only to the mature student of the Bible. Much will be advanced and different. We do not want to go to an extreme, as the people of Athens, of always wanting to hear only "some new thing" (Acts 17:21). But once a person has advanced several grades in school, he does not want to go back to grade one. We are admonished in the scriptures: "Let us go on..." (Heb. 6:1). I believe new things — things not noticed before — will be brought to light for every reader in this book about the Book of books.

Chapter 1

"IN THE BEGINNING GOD..."

It was 7:51 a.m. (EST), December 21, 1968. Apollo 8 sucessfully lifted off to begin its historic voyage. Traveling at nearly 25,000 miles an hour, the spacecraft hurled itself from the orbit of the earth and into flight toward the moon. Later, with the  attention of the world focused on them, the men aboard—Frank Borman, James A. Lovell Jr., and William A. Anders— each took part in reading Genesis 1:1-10, the story of creation. Anders began the reading with the opening words of the Bible: "In the beginning God..." These words were included on the stamp that was issued to commemorate this mission, with the moon surface below and planet earth— nearly a quarter of a million miles away— shining brightly in the darkness of space.

For us, what better place could there be to begin this book concerning the Bible than at the *beginning*? So we, too, turn to Genesis. Its name means the book of beginnings. An interesting example of word formation is seen by comparing the letters g-e-n in Genesis with words such as genes, geneology, generation, or generate, all of which also carry the meaning of "beginning."

Following the verses about the creation of heaven and earth, one does not read too far until he is introduced to Adam, then Eve, the garden of Eden, and the failure of the first human pair to obey the command of God. All trees were given to them for food, but of the tree of the knowledge of good and evil they were not to eat. It is not our purpose here to argue literal or figurative explanations against each other as to what this forbidden fruit may have been. Some say it was a pomegranate, figs (because of the mention of fig leaves), an apricot, or the traditional apple. But for now we will simply say that whatever it was, it involved a test of *obedience*—and Adam and Eve failed the test!

It is commonly assumed that when Eve ate of the forbidden fruit (at the suggestion of the serpent), that Adam was somewhere else. Then *later*, when he returned, he also ate of this fruit. But the fact is, Adam was *right there with her*! "And when the woman saw that the tree was good for food . . . she took of the fruit thereof, and did eat, and gave also unto her husband WITH HER; and he did eat" (Genesis 3:6).

Now I ask you: was her husband there "with her" or not? Yes, he was. So, men, we cannot blame all the trouble in the world on women! There is no indication that Adam tried to stop her and no indication that he was somewhere else at the time!

The result of them both eating this fruit was this: "And the eyes of them BOTH were opened, and they knew they were naked" (Gen. 3:7). It does not say her eyes were opened first, and his at some later time. No, the transgression involved "both" of them.

The idea that the forbidden fruit was an apple may have developed from the fact that in Latin the word which means "evil"—*malum*—is exactly the same word as "apple." Jerome translated the Bible into Latin in 405 A.D. and the idea may have passed on down from that time. But the Bible does not mention the apple in this connection. Nevertheless, some have pictured Eve eating an apple first; then later when Adam discovered what had happened, he was so shocked that a big lump came up in his throat. And that's why men have an Adam's apple to this day!

THE FALL—A SURPRISE TO GOD?

Others hold an idea that is even more silly; they somehow suppose that the fall was even a surprise to *God*! They suppose the serpent sneaked into the garden when God's back was turned—as though He who sees all things could not see this! Then, some would have us believe, when God came into the garden for his walk, he was horrified! Surprised! Shocked! His creation had fallen into sin! But the fall in Eden was no surprise to God.

First of all, man was made *weak*—as proven by the fact that all have sinned and come short of the glory of God. Adding to this, God placed the forbidden tree—not in some inaccessible thicket or remote part of the globe—but right in the *midst* of the garden

6

where it could be easily reached. With man's weak nature, with the tree of forbidden fruit right in the very center of the garden, and then with the serpent allowed to come in and carry out his work of temptation—surely God knew what would happen!

But there is actual scriptural proof that the fall in Eden was no surprise to God. This is clearly seen by the fact that even *before the foundation of the world* he planned out redemption in Jesus Christ! *Before* God ever created Adam and Eve, *before* the days of Eden, *before* any of these things, even *before* the foundation of the world itself—God already had a plan whereby fallen man could be redeemed! Salvation from sin is the result of "his own purpose and grace, which was given us in Christ Jesus BEFORE the world began" (2 Tim. 1:9). We are redeemed with the "precious blood of Christ...who verily was foreordained BEFORE the foundation of the world" (1 Peter 1:19, 20).

Since God planned out how men would be redeemed even before the foundation of the would, it is clear he KNEW man would fall and would be in need of this redemption.

A CONFERENCE IN HEAVEN?

Some believe that when the fall came in Eden, God called a great conference in heaven. All of the angels attended. God explained what had happened on earth. He asked for suggestions as to what could be done—some way to solve the problem. One angel suggested this, another that, but no plan was satisfactory. At this point, we are told, Jesus VOLUNTEERED to eventually go to earth and die for man. This plan was accepted and, consequently, a plan of salvation was made available to mankind.

What is wrong with this? It is wrong because the idea that Jesus "volunteered" is not correct. What happened at Calvary was no *last minute effort* to repair some damage that happened as a surprise to God! Total redemption was planned out in the divine mind "before the foundation of the world"; it was no last minute arrangement.

CAIN'S WIFE

The book of Job, which contains more *questions* [329] than any other book of the Bible, includes this question: "Art thou the first

7

man that was born?" (Job 15:7). Adam is referred to as "the first man" (1 Cor. 15:45), but he was not the first man *born* (Gen. 2:7). The first man that was born was Cain (Gen. 4:1). In verse 17 of this same chapter Cain's *wife* is mentioned. Because the Bible passes over some of these things quite rapidly, certain details are not even mentioned. Consequently, it is not uncommon for people to ask: "Where did Cain get his wife?"

When one preacher was asked this question by an infidel, he replied: "I don't know. When I get to heaven, I will ask him." "But what if Cain isn't in heaven?" To this the preacher replied: "Then *you* can ask him!"

According to *The Book of Jubilees*, a Jewish midrash (commentary) on Genesis and the first 14 chapters of Exodus written about 106 B.C., Cain married his sister. According to this book—for what it's worth—following the birth of Cain and Abel, Eve gave birth to two daughters: Awan and Azura. "And Cain took Awan his sister to be his wife and she bare him Enoch", while Seth married Azura his sister.

UNSCHOLARLY SAYINGS

The Biblical account of Adam and Eve has been the subject of numerous sayings—inaccurate and unscholarly— yet which are a definite part of the folklore of rural America:

At what time of day was Adam created? A little before Eve (Gen. 2:7, 21, 22).

What day of Adam's life was the longest? The first, because it had no Eve.

Who stopped Adam and Eve from gambling? God, when he took their paradise (pair o' dice) away from them (Gen. 3:23).

It wasn't the apple on the tree that caused the trouble; it was the pair (pear) on the ground.

Why, after making all other creatures, did God make woman last? He didn't want any advice.

What did Adam and Eve do when they were driven out of

Eden? They raised Cain (Gen. 3:23, 4:1).

What were Adam's first words to Eve, which can be spelled forward or backwards and say the same thing? "Madam I'm Adam."

Other similar sayings regarding Bible characters range from, "We know Joseph played tennis, because he served in Pharoah's courts", to "Peter was the smallest disciple because he slept on his watch."

RAIN BEFORE FLOOD?

It has sometimes been assumed that there was no rain upon the earth until the days of the flood. Sermons have told about Noah working for 120 years building the ark—all of which made him appear as a complete religious fanatic in the eyes of others, especially since it had never rained! But is this what the Bible says? The Biblical passage which is quoted in support of this view is Genesis 2:4-6:

"These are the generations of the heavens and of the earth when they were created, in the day that the Lord God made the earth and the heavens, and every plant of the field before it was in the earth, and every herb of the field before it grew: *for the Lord God has not caused it to rain upon the earth,* and there was not a man to till the ground. But there went up a mist from the earth, and watered the whole face of the ground . . . ."

This passage describes the condition of things *before* there was a man to till the ground. It was at *this time* that it had not rained upon the earth. Would this necessarily prove it did not rain after the Lord God made man? Can this passage prove it did not rain until the days of the flood which was 1,656 years later?

What this passage says is simply this: there was a time when the Lord had not caused it to rain on the earth. It also says there was no man and that plants were not growing yet. But soon the plants did grow. Soon there was a man on earth—as mentioned in the next verse. Though the Bible does not tell us, in so many words, *when* it first began to rain, we believe it is stretching the point to teach that it did not start raining until 1,656 years later—not until the time of the flood.

THE ARK—DID IT TAKE 120 YEARS TO BUILD?

Did it take Noah 120 years to build the ark? The mention of 120 years in Genesis 6:3 says nothing about the time required to build the ark. Instead, this verse says: "And the Lord said, My spirit shall not always strive with man, for that he also is flesh: yet his days shall be an hundred and twenty years." Judgment was pronounced upon mankind, but it was still 120 years away. Just *how* this judgment would be carried out was not, at this point, explained. Nothing was said about a flood or building an ark *at this time*.

One hundred and twenty years before the flood, Noah would have been 480 years old (for he was 600 at the time of the flood—Genesis 7:11). Noah's sons were not born until he was 500 years old (Gen. 5:32). It was not until quite some time *after* this that Noah was told to build the ark, for when Noah was told to do this, *his sons had grown up and married.* "Make thee an ark . . . I do bring a flood of waters upon the earth, to destroy all flesh . . . and thou shalt come into the ark, thou, *and thy sons*, and thy wife, *and thy sons' wives with thee*" (Gen. 6:14-18).

Since it is definitely implied that Noah's sons were grown and married when he was instructed to build the ark, and considering the ages of Noah and his sons, it seems clear that Noah was not working on the ark for 120 years. It is possible that the legend handed down in the book of Jasher is correct. According to this, it took five years to build the ark, but the Bible itself does not say how many years it took.

Question: When was a rooster's crow heard by every living creature on earth? (Answer: In Noah's ark (Gen. 7:13-23).)

"And the ark rested . . . upon the mountains of Ararat" (Gen. 8:4). No *specific* mountain is named here. There is no mention of a "Mount Ararat." Instead, "the mountains of Ararat" implies a region or nation within which these mountains were located. Ararat was the name of a country, a kingdom, as may be seen from Jeremiah 51:27: " . . . prepare the nations against her [Babylon], call together against her the kingdoms of Ararat, Minni, and Ashchenaz."

The two sons of Sennacherib "escaped into the land of Aramenia" (2 Kings 19:37). The word translated Armenia is the *same* word translated Ararat. Either word is correct, for Armenia is simply the later name by which Ararat was known.

CURSE ON HAM?

After the flood, Noah pronounced a curse on his son Ham. Or did he? The Bible does not say he did. Yet for some reason this is commonly assumed. As a result of this assumption, various ideas have been presented as to *what* this curse may have been.

Here is what the passage under consideration actually says:

"And Noah...planted a vineyard: and he drank of the wine, and was drunken; and he was uncovered within his tent. And Ham, the father of Canaan, saw the nakedness of his father, and told his two brethren without. And Shem and Japeth took a garment, and laid it upon both their shoulders, and went backward, and covered the nakedness of their father; and their faces were backward, and they saw not their father's nakedness. And Noah awoke from his wine, and he knew what his younger son had done unto him. And he said, Cursed be CANAAN; a servant of servants shall he be unto his brethren" (Gen. 9:20-27).

So, it was upon Canaan (*not* Ham) that the curse was pronounced.

This passage raises several questions. If Ham was the one that did wrong, why was the curse pronounced upon his son? Does the son bear the iniquity of the father? If Noah was wrong in becoming drunk, who was he to pronounce a curse on anyone? Was there any authority in his curse? Or was his cursing only an expression of his feelings when he awoke from his wine? Are we to conclude from this that it is morally wrong if a son happens to see his father without clothes? Why didn't Noah have the tent opening secured against entry?

Some feel there was more involved than what is stated. Some have quoted, for example, Leviticus 20:11: "And the man that lieth with his father's wife hath uncovered his father's nakedness." According to this verse, if Ham had committed incest with his father's wife, he had uncovered "his father's nakedness." While there is a similarity in wording here, this does not seem to have been the case in Genesis 9. The nakedness was

11

that of Noah himself. The one that was drunken was the one that was uncovered (Gen. 9:21).

Others believe that Ham did not merely look on his nude father, but actually *did* something to him, possibly a homosexual act.

Rashi (Solomon ben Isaac, 1040-1105 A.D.), an often-quoted Jewish commentator on the Bible and Talmud, said that Ham castrated Noah. I see no reason to believe this, though there is no account of Noah having any more children after this time.

Actually, the text does not say that Ham did anything other than see his father's nakedness and tell his brothers about it. We can *speculate* that he may have attempted to make a mockery of the nakedness, that he spoke against his father, that he refused to cover him, that he involved his son Canaan in his actions (whatever they were), or that he committed a homosexual act. But again, *the text does not say any of these things.*

I suppose the reason some believe Ham must have done something severe is because the curse sounds severe. However, was this curse even valid? Is there any reason to believe that the curse pronounced upon Ham's son ever became a reality?

Here is a man—over 600 years old, according to the Bible—who awakes from being dead drunk. He hollers out words of cursing—but instead of pronouncing the curse upon Ham who had seen his nakedness, he curses Ham's son Canaan—who may have been only a baby at this time! As far as the text is concerned, it would appear that Noah was in the wrong as much as anyone—after all *he* is the one that became drunk and uncovered in his tent. Whatever Ham did (or didn't do) would not seem reason for a curse to be put on his son Canaan.

In view of the many questions that surround Noah placing a curse on Ham's son, we believe the serious student of the Bible should keep everything in proper perspective. To believe a *whole race* is doomed to slavery because thousands of years ago someone saw the nakedness of his drunken father—as some contend—is, in my opinion, not only untrue, it is silly.

IT IS RECORDED IN THE BIBLE

The reason some believe Noah's curse to be valid is because it is recorded in the Bible. But the Bible records many things—even the words of Satan on occasions (Job 1:7). The Bible even says: "Curse God and die" (Job 2:9), but these were the words of Job's wife—not a message from God.

There are other statements in the Bible, statements which may contain *some* truth, but were never intended as verses upon which doctrines would be built. We will give four short examples.

(1) "We know that God heareth not sinners." (John 9:31). These were not the inspired words of a prophet or apostle. These were the words of the blind man who had been healed by Jesus, words given under questioning. At this point he did not even know Jesus was the son of God (see verses 35, 36). We know it is the prayer of a *righteous* man that availeth with God (James 5:16). However, did not God hear the prayer of the man who said: "God be merciful to me a sinner?" Yes, he did (Lk. 18:13, 14). To say that God never, under any circumstances, hears the prayer of a sinner is certainly *not* true.

(2) "How can I, except some man should guide me?" (Acts 8:31). These were the words of the Ethiopian official when Philip had asked him if he understood what he read from the book of Isaiah. There was a time when this verse was quoted to show that the common people could not understand the Bible; that it must be explained by the priest. But, again, these were the words of a man before he was converted. These can be no basis for doctrine. For while God has placed teachers in his church (Eph. 4:11), certainly we should not limit God as though he cannot directly open a truth to an individual (cf. 1 John 2:27). It would be a narrow viewpoint indeed to deny that someone all alone could not read from a Bible, understand what he reads, and be touched by God.

(3) "No man can do these miracles...except God be with him" (John 3:2). Some years ago there was a radio program which used the following words as an introduction to the evangelist who was about to speak: "...Jesus said, 'No man can do these miracles except God be with him'..." But it was *Nicodemus* who said this, *not Jesus*! There is an element of truth in the words of Nicodemus on this occasion, for Jesus spoke of certain miracles

13

as a confirmation of his divine mission (John 14:11). But a statement made by a man who did not, at that point, understand about being born again would definitely have to be qualified by other verses.

(4) "For if this counsel or this work be of men, it will come to nought: but if it be of God, ye cannot overthrow it; lest haply ye be found even to fight against God" (Acts 5:38, 39). The man who said this was Gamaliel, a noted doctor of the law among Jews, and under whom Paul, before his conversion, had been taught (Acts 22:3). Gamaliel cited the example of a cult of four hundred people who followed Theudas, but who was killed and his followers scattered. The same had been the fate of those who followed Judas of Galilee. With this background given to the Jewish council which sought to kill the apostles, Gamaliel gave the recommendation of the words we are considering. As a result the apostles were only punished and released.

But the words of Gamaliel, though recorded in the Bible, were never intended for doctrine. While there is some good logic in what he said, yet his statement is not *totally* true. He mentioned two cults which had been organized only to come to naught. He then made the statement that if a work is not of God it will come to naught also. But there are many groups, organizations, and religions which are *not of God*, yet have been in existence for centuries! The *length* of time that a group has been in existence does not, necessarily, mean it is the work of God.

AGES IN THE BIBLE

Looking again at the book of Genesis, we repeatedly read of various men who lived, their *ages* are given, and then we will read of each: ". . . and he died" (See Genesis 5). The ages of *men* are given, but what about *women*?

Of all the women mentioned in the Bible, an exact age at death has only been given for *one*: Sarah! "And Sarah was an hundred and seven and twenty years old . . . and Sarah died" (Gen. 23:1). In fact, so far as I have been able to determine, Sarah is the only woman for whom an *exact* age is given—not only at death, but at any point in life. The only exceptions might be the little daughter of Jarius who was age twelve (Mk. 5:42) and Anna, for whom an approximate age is given (Lk. 2:36, 37). Otherwise, Sarah stands out as an exception, her age being recorded in life and death.

Probably the reason the *age* of Sarah is specifically mentioned is because of the advanced age at which she gave birth to Isaac, a point that is mentioned several times in the Bible. When the promise of this child was given to Abraham, he laughed and said in his heart: "Shall Sarah, that is ninety years old, bear?" (Gen. 17:17). But Isaac was born to her at this advanced age.

According to a Jewish legend, there were some women who doubted that Sarah had actually given birth to Isaac. (They may have suspected that Isaac was the child of a slave girl, as had been the case with Ishmael.) If she had indeed given birth to Isaac, they wanted her to prove it by nursing their babies. She refused to do this and their doubts were confirmed. When Abraham heard this, he told Sarah: "Uncover your breasts and provide milk for this entire brood", which she did!

If this is a true account of events, it explains a verse which otherwise is quite obscure. Genesis 21:17 speaks of Sarah providing milk for children (plural), though she only had *one* son of her own. "And she said, Who would have said unto Abraham, that Sarah should have given CHILDREN suck? for I have born him a son in his old age."

ABRAHAM, ISAAC AND JACOB

As the Bible story continues, a number of chapters are devoted to events in the lives of the three patriarchs, Abraham, Isaac and Jacob. For years, Jacob believed his son Joseph had died, only to find out later he was alive and had obtained a prominent position in Egypt. A famine swept the land of Canaan and Jacob had to make a decision about moving down into Egypt. At this point he was given a promise: "Fear not to go down into Egypt...Joseph shall put his hand upon thine EYES" (Gen. 46:4), or as some versions have it: "And Joseph will close your eyes in peace."

To put one's hands upon the eyes was a custom in which the nearest of kin would close the eyes of a loved one at death. Thus Jacob was given the assurance that his son Joseph would be with him when he died. In view of this promise, he did not hesitate to journey to where Joseph was. He then lived in Egypt for seventeen years (Gen. 47:28). And, even as the prediction had revealed many years before, Joseph was there with Jacob when he died. "And Joseph fell upon his father's face, and wept upon him, and kissed him" (Gen. 50:1).

In the course of time, "there arose up a new king over Egypt, which knew not Joseph" and the children of Israel were forced into slavery (Exodus 1:8-12). Conditions grew worse for them until finally under the leadership of Moses, the "exodus" became a reality. It is from this fact that we have the name of the second book of the Bible, having the meaning of the people going forth. We can see in the word *exodus* similarities to some present day words. Notice the o-d in Exodus. In the car we have an odometer which measures the going forth of the car (mileage). The letters e-x in Exodus are clearly visible in words we used such as export and exit.

MOSES AND THE ETHIOPIAN WOMAN

Moses, who was used of God to bring the Israelites forth from Egypt, was married to an Ethiopian woman. Many have been puzzled about this. We recall that Miriam and Aaron—the sister and brother of Moses—had some differences with him "because of the Ethiopian woman whom he had married: for he had married an Ethiopian woman" (Num. 12:1). The details of this dispute are not given. What they did not like about this Ethiopian woman is not explained in the Bible.

Steven tells us that Moses, being raised in Pharaoh's household, was well-educated in the wisdom of the Egyptians and was mighty in *deeds* (Acts 7:22). Again, the Bible does not explain what these deeds were. But Josephus, the noted Jewish historian of the first century, fills in the details about the deeds of Moses and also the Ethiopian woman!

Egypt had become involved in a war with the Ethiopians. Moses was appointed general of the Egyptian army. He was very successful in this position, which explains how he was mighty in deeds. "He came upon the Ethiopians before they expected him; and, joining battle with them, he beat them, and deprived them of the hopes they had of success against the Egyptians, and went on in overthrowing their cities, and indeed made a great slaughter of

16

these Ethiopians" (Antiquities of the Jews, Book 2, 10:2).

Finally Moses and the Egyptian armies beseiged the royal city of Ethiopia called Saba. It was well fortified and difficult to take. This is where "the Ethiopian woman" comes into the picture. According to Josephus, her name was Tharbis, the daughter of the king. "She happened to see Moses as he led the army near the walls, and fought with great courage; and admiring the subtility of his undertakings, and believing him to be the author of the Egyptians' success...she fell deeply in love with him; and upon the prevalency of that passion, sent to him the most faithful of all her servants to discourse with him about their marriage. He thereupon accepted the offer, on condition she would procure the delivering up of the city...and that when he had once taken possession of the city, he would not break his oath to her. No sooner was the agreement made, but it took effect immediately; and when Moses had cut off the Ethiopians, he gave thanks to God, and consummated his marriage, and led the Egyptians back to their own land" (Antiquities of the Jews, Book 2, 10:2).

Irenaeus, an early church father, summed it up in these words: "When Moses was nourished in the king's palace, he was appointed general of the army against the Ethiopians, and conquered them, when he married that king's daughter; because, out of her affection for him, she delivered the city up to him."

MOSES KILLED AN EGYPTIAN—WHY?

Though he was raised up in Pharoah's house, Moses knew his roots were with the Hebrews. When he was forty, he went to visit his own people. Seeing one of them oppressed by an Egyptian taskmaster, he became angry, killed the Egyptian, and buried him in the sand. But why this particular Egyptian? All slaves were apparently oppressed, why was this one situation notable above others? Why did this one case enflame Moses into killing a man? There must have been some special reason. According to the book of Jasher, the Egyptian had raped the slave's wife:

"And when the man who was beaten saw Moses he ran to him for help...and he said to him...This Egyptian came to my house in the night, bound me, and came to my wife in my presence, and now he seeks to take my life away. And when Moses heard this wicked thing, his anger was kindled against the

17

Egyptian, and he turned this way and the other, and when he saw there was no man there he smote the Egyptian and hid him in the sand" (Jasher 71:2, 3).

Something else that is not well-known—and this point is explained in the Bible itself—is the *reason* why Moses came to visit his brethren at the age of forty. Having been "mighty in deeds" as an Egyptian military leader, Moses now wanted to help his own people. He wanted to help them escape from slavery, then

and there, and this was forty years before the actual exodus came! He thought the Hebrews would understand that *he* would be used by God to bring about their deliverance, but they did not understand this. Let me give you the scripture that spells this out. *"For* he supposed is brethren would have understood how that God *by his hand* would deliver them: but they understood not"* (Acts 7:25). Having killed a man, his efforts were rejected by the people, and he fled to the backside of the desert.

Forty years passed and Moses returned to Egypt, having received a divine directive at the burning bush. Moses was eighty years old now. But it was not time to *retire*; it was time to *re-fire*. Through mighty signs and wonders in Egypt, the deliverance of the people was secured and they escaped from slavery.

GIANTS IN THE LAND

Having escaped from Egypt, the journey in the wilderness was not without its problems. Twelve spies were sent into the promised land. Upon approaching Canaan, they found the wooded mountain infested with giants. "And all the people that we saw in it are men of great stature. And there we saw the giants, the sons of Anak, which came of the giants: and we were in our own sight as grasshoppers, and so we were in their sight" (Numbers 13:32, 33).

The Bible mentions "the valley of the giants" (Joshua 15:8) and another reference says: "That also was accounted a land of giants: giants dwelt therein in old time; and the Ammonites call them Zamzummims; a people great, and many, and tall" (Deut. 2:20, 21). In Second Samuel 21:20 we read about "a man of great stature, that had on every hand six fingers, and on every foot six toes, four and twenty in number; and he also was born to the giant." It is a rare situation, but a number of such cases have been recorded in history.

One giant mentioned in the Bible, King Og, had a real "king size" bed. Figuring a cubit at 18 inches, his bed was thirteen and a half feet in length and six feet wide (Deut. 3:11). Goliath, the most famous giant mentioned in the Bible, was about nine feet, nine inches tall. His armor weighed 156 pounds and his spearhead almost 19 pounds (1 Sam. 17.4-7).

Question: How many hard boiled eggs could the giant Goliath eat on an empty stomach?

Answer: One. After that, his stomach would no longer be empty.

19

RITUAL PROSTITUTION AT MOAB

What created a bigger problem for the Israelites in the wilderness than giants was their involvement with the *women* of Moab. "And Israel abode in Shittim, and the people began to commit *whoredom* with the daughters of Moab. And they called the people unto the sacrifices of their gods: and the people did eat, and bowed down to their gods. And Israel joined himself unto Baal-peor" (Numbers 25:1, 2).

Today we think of prostitution only in a secular sense. But at that time, it should be understood that prostitution was a part of the *religion* of Moab. It was *ritual* prostitution. Sexual acts were a part of their *worship* in honor of Baal-peor. So when the Israelites engaged in these acts, it was not only an involvement in immorality, but an immorality which was a part of the worship of other gods!

The reader will recall that Balaam was repeatedly shown that as long as the Isrelites obeyed God, they would be blessed and no enemy could defeat them (Numbers 22-24). Realizing this, Balaam figured if the Israelites would *disobey God,* God himself would judge them. The details of this are given in the *Biblical Antiquities of Philo:*

"Then Balaam said unto him [Balac]: Come and let us advise what thou shalt do to them. Choose out the most comely women that are among you and that are in Midian and set them before them naked, and adorned with gold and jewels, and it shall be when they shall see them and lie with them, they will sin against their Lord and fall into your hands, for otherwise thou canst not subdue them. And so saying Balaam turned away and returned to his place. And thereafter the people were led astray after the daughters of Moab, for Balac did all that Baalam had showed him" (Philo 18:13, 14).

With this background information, we can better understand Numbers 31:16: "Behold, these [women of Moab] caused the children of Israel, through the counsel of Balaam, to commit trespass against the Lord in the matter of Peor, and there was a plague among the congregation."

The story of Balaam is given in three chapters of Numbers (22-24). The involvement of Israel with the daughters of Moab is given in chapter 25. Balaam's part in this is not mentioned in these chapters and there is only a brief mention, as we have given, in Numbers 31:1. This point, recorded here and in *Philo*, however, is undisputed. The writer of Revelation 2:14 was familiar with this, for there we read of "Balaam, who taught Balac to cast a stumbling block before the children of Israel, to eat things sacrificed unto idols, *and to commit fornication.*"

The Old Testament seems to picture Balaam as being, at times, in actual communication with God. The New Testament verses which mention Balaam point out the error of his way. Some think he never was a true prophet of God, even though he said some good things, and others feel he started out good and went bad. Whatever, Balaam clearly knew that the Israelites would be blessed by God and would defeat their enemies. Yet Balaam's death came when he was on the side which he, himself, had said would be defeated! When the battle was over, among those slain was found the body of Balaam. "Balaam also, the son of Beor, the soothsayer, did the children of Israel slay with the sword among them that were slain" (Josh. 13:22).

QUOTATIONS FROM BALAAM

Two well-known Bible quotations are based on the words of Balaam. "God is not a man, that he should lie; neither the son of man, that he should repent: hath he said, and shall he not do it? or hath he spoken, and shall he not make it good?" (Numbers 23:19). These words are true—they provide a great preaching text—yet these were not the words of a recognized prophet of God, but of Balaam.

The other quotation from Balaam, "What hath God wrought!" was made famous because it formed the first message sent over the electric telegraph which was perfected and built by Samuel F. B. Morse. The first telegraph line, constructed with $30,000 appropriated by Congress in 1834, was completed in the spring of 1844 and ran between Washington, D.C. and Baltimore, Maryland.

The quotation, "What hath God wrought!" was chosen by Annie Ellsworth, daughter of the commissioner of patents, the complete text of which says: "Surely there is no enchantment against Jacob, neither is there any divination against Israel: according to this time it shall be said to Jacob and of Israel, What hath God wrought!" (Num. 23:23).

CLOTHING MIRACLE?

For the forty years that the Israelites wandered in the wilderness, we are told that their clothes did not get old upon their bodies and their shoes did not get old on their feet. The three following verses are the ones which mention this:

"Thy raiment waxed not old upon thee, neither did thy foot swell, these forty years" (Deut. 8:4). "Your clothes are not waxen old upon you, and thy shoe is not waxen old upon they foot" (Deut. 29:5). "Forty years didst thou sustain them in the wilderness, so that they lacked nothing; their clothes waxed not old, and their feet swelled not" (Neh. 9:1).

In other words, during the forty years in the wilderness, they did not have to wear old clothes or old shoes. Does this necessarily imply that their clothing and shoes never wore out? Are we to assume from this that their clothing and shoes were miraculously preserved, so that after forty years they were still wearing the *same* clothes and shoes?

On this point, Adam Clarke has stated in his noted commentary (Vol. 1 p. 760) the following: "The plain meaning of this much-tortured text appears to me to be this: 'God so amply provided for them all the necessaries of life, that they never were obliged to wear tattered garments, nor were their feet injured for lack of shoes or sandals." He goes on to mention that there were various workers, carvers, jewelers, weavers, etc.,

22

among the Israelites at this period. He says there is no reason to believe they did not have shoe cobblers and tailors also.

That they had the *ability*, *materials*, and did in fact *make clothes* during this time can be seen in the case of the priestly garments: "And these are the garments which they shall make; a breastplate, and an ephod, and a robe, and a broidered coat, a mitre, and a girdle: and they shall make holy garments for Aaron . . . shall take gold, and blue, and purple, and scarlet, and fine linen" (Exodus 28:1-5).

Instead of the idea that the Israelites wore the same clothes for forty years and such were miraculously preserved, the Barnes commentary (p. 287) states: "They had clothes, it would seem, in abundance (Exodus 12:34, 35) at the beginning of the forty years; and during those years they had many sheep and oxen, and so must have had much material for clothing always at command. No doubt also they carried on a traffic in these, as in other commodities, with the Moabites and the nomadic tribes of the desert. Such ordinary supplies must not be shut out of consideration, even if they were on occasions supplemented by extraordinary providences of God, as was undoubtedly the case with their food."

If, as some have assumed, the Israelites wore the *same* clothes for forty years, what about the clothing of babies? With the exception of Joshua and Caleb, all who entered the promised land were under twenty years of age when leaving Egypt or were born during the forty years. This means that the vast majority of people who entered the promised land would have had clothes that miraculously *stretched*—according to the belief. No less than 600,000 males born during this period would have had garments that were not only miraculously preserved, but which also miraculously stretched as they grew from infancy to adulthood.

Picture, if you will, a baby that was born just before the Israelites left Egypt. Its mother makes a tiny garment for it. Are we to believe that ten years later this child is wearing the *same* garment, only now it has stretched to fit a ten-year-old? At forty years of age, when entering the promised land, was he still wearing the same garment? We do not doubt that with God all things are possible, but is this really the meaning here? Would this even be desirable—no change, just the same garment all those years? If the clothing miraculously stretched, why, we question, is this not mentioned, since this would be a greater miracle?

23

Here is what Clarke says in summary: "It is generally supposed that God, by a miracle, preserved their clothes from wearing out: but if this sense be admitted, it will require, not one miracle, but a chain of the most successive and astonishing miracles ever wrought... It would imply, that the clothes of the infant grew up with the increase of his body to manhood, which would require a miracle to be continually wrought on every thread, and on every particle of matter of which that thread was composed... No such miraculous interference was necessary."

The Bible says their clothes did not wear out upon them; that is, they did not have to wear old clothing. Their shoes did not wear out upon their feet; that is, they did not have to wear worn-out shoes. Their feet did not swell—from cuts and bruises—which would have happened had they not had proper shoes. The miraculous element is in the fact that they were supplied with the necessary things—*even in the wilderness*. God took care of them.

I have given here what I feel is the best explanation. I do not present it as dogma and have no quarrel with any who may feel otherwise.

*   *   *   *   *

There were two churches in the small prairie town: the Baptist and the Methodist. Neither church was large enough to support a full time pastor, so a merger was planned. It seemed like a good idea and all was going well until the question came up as to what name they would call this church. Instead of using one of the former names, a new name seemed to be in order. One man suggested that they simply call it the Christian church. Everyone agreed with this suggestion. Well, everyone, that is, except one lady. "I've been a Baptist for 30 years", she exclaimed, "you're not about to make a *Christian* out of me!"

*   *   *   *   *

Seven days without prayer makes one weak.

Chapter 2

THE FOODS OF THE BIBLE

It is sometimes assumed that the children of Israel ate *only* manna during the forty years in the wilderness. A study of the books which cover this period—Exodus, Leviticus, Numbers, and Deuteronomy—however, shows that they had other food to eat in addition to the manna.

"The children of Israel did eat manna forty years" (Exodus 16:35). But as the Barnes commentary says: "This does not necessarily imply that the Israelites were fed *exclusively* on manna...They had numerous flocks and herds...which gave them milk, cheese, and of course a limited supply of flesh: nor is there any reason to suppose that during a considerable part of that time they may not have cultivated some spots of fertile ground in the wilderness. We may assume, as in most cases of miracle, that the supernatural supply was commensurate with their actual necessity."

They began receiving the manna shortly after they came out of Egypt (Exodus 16). Yet, in the first month of the second year after coming out of Egypt, they kept the passover, eating lamb and unleavened bread and bitter herbs (Numbers 9). At the close of the forty years, "the children of Israel...kept the passover...and they did eat of the old corn of the land on the morrow after the passover, unleavened cakes, and parched corn...and the manna ceased on the morrow after they had eaten of the old corn of the land" (Joshua 5:10-12). From these references we see that while receiving the manna, certain other foods were eaten in connection with the passover.

We also know that as they passed through certain lands, such as the land of Esau, they were instructed: "Ye shall buy *meat* of them for money, that ye may *eat*; and ye shall also buy water of them for money, that ye may drink" (Deut. 2:6, 7). If manna was the only food they were to eat, these instructions about buying food would have been completely out of place!

Moses sent a message to the king of Heshbon. "Thou shalt sell me *meat* for money, that I may *eat*...as the children of Esau...and the Moabites did unto me...Until I shall pass over Jordan into the land which the Lord our God giveth us" (Deut. 2:69). Again, why would he speak of buying food from them if their diet was limited to manna?

A VALID COMPLAINT?

On one occasion, it is true, they complained of having only manna. "There is nothing at all, beside this manna, before our eyes" (Numbers 11:6). But how valid was this complaint? Was it absolutely true that they had nothing other than manna? Or were they simply hungry for certain meats, fish, cucumbers, melons, leeks, onions, and garlick that had been a part of their Egyptian diet? (cf. verse 5). They were given quails to eat at this time; but the Lord was dispeased with their complaining.

That they had other food available to them during the forty years—either all or part of the time—is seen in the mention of various foods that were used in their offerings. Flour, oil, honey, salt and corn are mentioned in Leviticus 2:1-14. They had "a very great multitude of cattle" (Num. 32:1; Deut. 3:19). Those that were without blemish were used in their various sacrifices (Lev. 1). The priests ate meat from the sacrifices (Lev. 6:16; 8:31).

Moses instructed the people not to eat the fat or the blood of an ox, sheep, or goat (Lev. 7:23-26), implying, of course, that they did eat the *meat*. Furthermore, it was during this time that the Israelites were told what meats to eat and which meats should not be eaten. "These are the beasts which ye shall eat..." (Lev. 1:2). If their entire diet during those forty years was only manna, explaining which meats were clean or unclean unto them would have been without purpose. If the manna was the only thing God wanted them to eat, he would have told them to eat no meat at all! But, instead, he explained *which* meats they were to eat!

It was also during this time that God gave regulations about the Nazarite vow. "When either man or woman"—notice that a *woman* could become a Nazarite—"shall separate themselves to vow a vow of a Nazarite...he shall separate himself from wine...neither shall he eat moist grapes, or dried...he shall eat nothing that is made of the vine tree, from the kernels even to the husk" (Num. 6:2-4). Why would such regulations about diet be given if the only thing anyone was eating was manna? If *none* of the people were eating these things, such food prohibitions for the Nazarites would have been without meaning.

Mention is made of the people eating grapes and corn (Deut. 23:24, 25). The spies brought back grapes, pomegranates, and figs (Numbers 13:23). During the forty years God supplied the Israelites with manna which served as their "bread", as it was called, but there is no reason to believe this was the *only* food they had during this time.

BIBLICAL RECIPE

Many different food products are mentioned in the Bible. Someone has even written a recipe using Bible verses!

Old Fashioned Scripture Cake

2 cups Jeremiah 6:20

1 cup Judges 5:25 (last clause)

6 Jeremiah 17:11

2 cups 1 Samuel 30:12

2 cups Nahum 3:12

2 cups Numbers 17:8

2 tablespoons 1 Samuel 14:25

½ cup Judges 4:19 (last clause)

4 ½ cups 1 Kings 4:22

Pinch of Leviticus 2:13

2 teaspoons Luke 13:21

Season with 2 Chronicles 9:9

Mix and bake till done.

MILK

The word "milk" today causes most of us to think of milk from cows. But most of the milk mentioned in the Bible came from goats, sheep, or camels. In a few references in the King James Version, the older spelling for milk (milch) still remains. Jacob, for example, offered "thirty milch camels" as a present to Esau (Gen. 32:15).

I met a preacher once who never would be without goats' milk. He traveled here and there preaching, pulling a trailer with his goats behind his car. Proverbs 27:27 was quoted in this connection: "And thou shalt have goats' milk enough for thy food, for the food of thy household."

Interestingly enough, according to scientific tests, the milk with the most nutrition is neither that of humans, goats, cows, or camels, but the milk of *seals*.

"Every body needs milk", says an advertising slogan. But every body does not need milk. The *Dictionary of Misinformation* (p. 155) points out that many people do not possess the enzyme by which milk is digested. For such people, milk induces diarrhea.

"VENISON"—MISUNDERSTOOD

The word "venison" has been commonly misunderstood. This word appears in the Bible a total of eight times, all of which are in connection with Esau and Jacob (Genesis 27). In order to obtain the blessing of their elderly and blind father, each son brought him a portion of meat. Esau went to hunt for venison, we are told, but Jacob killed two kids of the goats from the family flock. It is not necessary to repeat the details of the story here, except to point out that it is a common mistake to suppose that Esau went out to hunt a *deer* while Jacob offered goat meat.

Probably each son presented the flesh of young *goats*, Jacob's being that of a domestic kid, while that of Esau was a wild kid. When the King James Version was translated, "venison" was applied to the flesh of *any* wild animal killed by hunting and used for food. The word is derived from the Latin *venation*, meaning "hunting." It was applied to the flesh of wild boars, hares, deer,

28

pheasants, ducks, geese, quail and other game animals and birds. Limiting this word to the flesh of the deer kind is a comparatively recent development. It came about because the deer became the most important game animal in England and this usage has been passed on to us.

"CORN"—ITS BIBLICAL MEANING

The word "corn" in the Bible has commonly also been misunderstood. We read that Jesus and his disciples picked corn as they "went through the corn fields" (Mk. 2:23). These were actually wheat or grain fields. They never once saw what *we* call corn fields.

What we call corn (maize or Indian corn) was probably native to South America and was not known by Europeans until a few centuries ago when they discovered it in the Americas. The word "corn", in much of the world, has long been used to denote any of the small seeded cereals such as barley, wheat, and rye. It is used in a specific sense in various countries for whichever cereal grain is most prominent. In England, corn is wheat; in the Scandinavian countries it is barley; in most parts of Germany it is rye; in the United States, maize—corn that grows on the cob. These things can be easily verified in almost any encyclopedia.

"HUSKS"—NOT CORN HUSKS

In the story of the wayward son (commonly called the "prodigal son", though this expression does not appear in the Bible), some have thought he became so hungry in the "far country" that he *ate the husks* which were given to feed the swine. But the story does not say this. In his hunger, we are told, "he would fain [gladly] have filled his belly with the *husks* that the swine did eat", but he came to

29

himself and returned to his father's house.

Just what these "husks" were has also been commonly misunderstood. We know it was not the outward covering of the corn (maize) we are familiar with; it was not corn husks. The accompanying words from the commentary by Barnes (p. 103) will explain: "The 'husks'—a mistranslation—are fleshy pods, somewhat like those of the locust-tree, from six to ten inches long and one broad, laid inside with a gelatinous substance, not wholly unpleasant to the taste when thoroughly ripe . . . it is still the food which the swine do eat . . . The cut will give an idea of these pods, or husks, as they are called in our translation."

FOOD COLLECTION AT CORINTH

Paul wrote to the Corinthians concerning a food collection for the saints who were suffering from famine in Jerusalem. That such was a *food* collection has sometimes been overlooked as one reads First Corinthians 16:1-4. "Now concerning the collection *for the saints* . . . upon the first day of the week let every one of you lay by him in store, as God hath prospered him, that there be no *gatherings* when I come. And when I come, whomsoever ye shall approve by your letters, *them* will I send to bring your liberality unto *Jerusalem*. And if it be meet that I go also, they shall go with me."

The saints in Jerusalem had a need—probably not so much for money as for food (cf. Acts 11:28-30). Because it was a contribution of food, we can understand why Paul told them to go ahead and store it up so it would not have to be gathered when he got there. Being a contribution of food, we can also understand why several people would be needed to take it from Corinth to Jerusalem.

In reference to this very collection, Paul wrote to the Christians at Rome that he was going "unto Jerusalem to minister unto the saints. For it hath pleased them of Macedonia and *Achaia* [this is where the Corinthian church was located—2 Cor. 1:1; Acts 18:1, 12] to make a certain contribution for the poor saints which are at Jerusalem . . . When therefore I have performed this, and have sealed to them this *fruit*, I will come by you into Spain" (Rom. 15:24-28).

In this passage, Paul specifically mentions fruit. Without modern methods of preserving food, I believe the fruit that was sent to Jerusalem was *dried* fruit. Raisins were no doubt sent from Corinth, such being one of the main products of that area. The word *currant*, according to the dictionary, comes from "raisins de Corinthe, raisins of Corinth, currants, from Corinth in Greece, whence, probably, the raisins were first imported . . . 1. A small seedless raisin." Thus we see that Corinth was especially known for this product. The port of Corinth is still a center for the export of various fruits, including currants.

BREAD AND GRAPE JUICE?

Several years ago I spoke with a man who told me that he ate only bread and grape juice. Nothing but bread and grape juice! Why? He said that this is what Jesus gave his disciples to eat and so this is what we should eat—nothing else. There was nothing I could say that would make him think any differently. He was frail and in very poor physical (and mental) condition.

I have heard of people who would not eat potatoes because this word is not in the Bible. But this omission proves nothing, for potatoes were not even known in the land of the Bible during the centuries it was being written.

Various ideas exist about the origin of the potato, but it is generally agreed that the white potato originated in Peru. From here Spanish explorers introduced it into Spain. It was not accepted in Europe as a regular part of the diet until the 19th century!

To refuse to eat potatoes just because this word does not appear in the Bible would be like refusing to eat ice cream or hamburgers simply because these things are not mentioned. I know of some who eat hamburgers, but prefer calling them beefburgers rather than *ham*-burgers. Others, who feel they should not eat *any* meat, use meat substitutes such as those made with soybeans.

The meatless diet was the belief of John Harvey Kellogg, who along with Ellen G. White, stressed this in their sanitarium built at Battle Creek, Michigan, in 1866. Patients flocked to the sanitarium which also stressed sunlight, fresh air, proper rest, and natural methods as health factors. But the meatless menu proved monotonous to many of the patients who were not accustomed to a vegetarian diet. It is said that some of the patients would sneak across the street to a shanty restaurant called "The Red Onion" for an occasional illegal steak!

But the vegetarian idea worked out well for Kellogg. He began to experiment with meat substitutes. In the course of things he invented corn flakes and other breakfast cereals. Today these products are widely used. Who hasn't heard of Kellogg's Corn Flakes of Battle Creek?

It worked out well for Charles Post, too. While a wheelchair patient at the Battle Creek Sanitarium, he became interested in Kellogg's experiments. As a result, he invented a coffee substitute which he named *Postum* and a breakfast cereal which he also named after himself: *Post Toasties*. He made a fortune with these products.

SOFT DRINKS

Another tremendous success story centers on the use of carbonated water in soft drinks. It is interesting to note that the man who invented or discovered carbonated water—Joseph Priestly (1733-1804)—was not only a noted scientist, but also a *preacher*. In 1767 he was called to be the minister of Mill Hill Chapel near Leeds, England. Little did he realize that some day products with carbonated water would be used world-wide, drinks like *Coca-Cola*.

The original syrup for *Coca-Cola* was developed by Major John Pemberton on May 8, 1886. Carbonated water was later added and the product which resulted provides a fantastic success story in advertising and marketing. We might suppose that *Coca-Cola* is the oldest soft drink in existence. However, *Dr. Pepper* began to be sold on a commercial basis as early as 1885. Though for years it was only a regional drink—originating in Waco, Texas—it is now widely used and is the *oldest* name brand soft drink in the world. The man who originated this drink named it after his father-in-law who was indeed a doctor, Dr. Pepper.

What we know as *7 Up* came later and dates back to October, 1929. It was originally called *Bib-label Lithiated Lemon Lime*

Soda! A few times over the years I have preached a message on "7 Up", not the Un-Cola, but what we might call the seven "ups" of the Bible. A brief outline of this message with its seven points and accompanying scriptures follows:

1. Wake up. (Ephesians 5:14).

2. Look up. (Luke 21:28).

3. Pay up. (Matt. 6:21).

4. Make up. (Matt. 5:24).

5. Fire up. (Rev. 3:15, 16).

6. Shut up. (James 1:19).

7. Cheer up. (Acts 27:25).

*   *   *   *   *

A church at which I spoke some years ago had a glass of water on the pulpit. I don't normally drink water when speaking, but since it was there for me, I took a drink. The water tasted strange. I found out later that a week or so before there had been some flowers in this glass. Someone had dumped out the flowers, but had forgotten to empty the water they were in!

*   *   *   *   *

I heard a preacher say one time: "Would someone please bring a glass of water to the pulpit for me? I feel a *dry* sermon coming on." He was a noted preacher—he always preached from notes.

*   *   *   *   *

The story is told of a minister who called a meeting of the board to be held right after the morning service. The various board members all met in a certain room, along with one other man. The pastor found it necessary to explain that this meeting was only for the board. To this the man replied that he was as *bored* as any of the other members!

CHAPTER 3

LITTLE-KNOWN FACTS
ABOUT WELL-KNOWN PEOPLE

Dale Carnegie once wrote a book using the title we have chosen for this chapter. His book included short stories about Albert Einstein, Orville Wright, Carrie Nation, Robert Ripley, Aimee Semple McPherson, Upton Sinclair, Walt Disney, Brigham Young, F. W. Woolworth, and others.

In the Bible, there are persons who are well-known, yet there are details about them which are not well-known. Joseph, for example, who was sold by his brothers into Egyptian slavery, is a well-known Bible character. We know about his rise from slavery to a position of prominence in Egypt and of his noble life. Usually we have thought of his record as spotless. Yet, there is one point about him that is not well-known. According to Genesis 44:5, Joseph practiced *divination*. Specific mention is made of a silver cup which he used for this purpose. Just how this was done, we are not told. We do know that divination, at least in a later period of Hebrew history, was strongly condemned (Deut. 18:10, 14).

ZEDEKIAH, KING OF JUDAH

Two unusual prophecies were given concerning Zedekiah. Through Ezekiel, a prophecy said he would be taken "to Babylon to the land of the Chaldeans; *yet shall he not see it*, though he shall die there" (Ezekiel 12:13). Another prophecy, this one given by Jeremiah, said he would "surely be delivered into the hand of the king of Babylon, and shall speak with him mouth to mouth, and his *eyes* shall behold his eyes" (Jer. 32:4).

According to these prophecies, Zedekiah would be delivered into the hand of the king of Babylon, with whom he would speak eye to eye. He would be taken into Babylon. He would not see Babylon. He would die in Babylon. Such phrases seem almost contradictory. But the history of what actually happened makes it clear.

"The army of the Chaldeans pursued after the king, and over

took Zedekiah in the plains of Jericho; and all his army was scattered from him. Then they took the king, and carried him up unto the king of Babylon to Riblah in the land of Hamath; where he gave judgment upon him. And the king of Babylon slew the sons of Zedekiah·before his eyes...Then he PUT OUT THE EYES OF ZEDEKIAH; and the king of Babylon bound him in chains, and carried him to Babylon, and put him in prison till the day of his death" (Jer. 52:4-11).

Thus Zedekiah was taken captive and did see the king of Babylon. His eyes were then put out and he was led into Babylon where he died. This explains the prophecies he had been given in warning. He was indeed taken to Babylon—and died there—yet he did not SEE it.

PETER THE FISHERMAN

Jesus told Peter, "Launch out into the deep, and let down your *nets* for a draught" (Luke 5:4). Notice that the word "nets" is *plural.* Peter explained that they had fished all night in those waters and had taken nothing. "Nevertheless", he said, "at thy word I will let down the *net*" (verse 5). Notice that Peter used the *singular*—"net." This is *not* what Jesus said!

It ended up that Peter and the others "inclosed a great multitude of fishes: and their net brake." Had Peter followed the instructions of Jesus more carefully, had he used "nets" and not just a "net", certain problems would have been avoided. Of course, the overall point of this incident was to illustrate how these men would, through Christ, become fishers of *men*. But this passage also shows how it is possible to pass over certain details in our study of the Bible—in this case, failing to see a contrast that becomes apparent once we notice the word "nets" used by Jesus and the word "net" in Peter's reply,

After the resurrection of Christ, Peter was again involved in a fishing incident. After following the instructions of Jesus, he caught "an hundred and fifty and three" large fish (John 21:11). Then follows the noted passage in which Jesus asked Peter: "Lovest thou me more than these?"—more than these 153 fish.

Because John recorded an exact number regarding these fish—153 (not "about" 153)—some have felt this number must have a deeper meaning, an idea which has given rise to quite a bit of speculation. I present the following "solutions" only because they may be of general interest to the reader:

Some believe there were 153 nations at the time. When Jesus asked Peter if he loved him more than these 153 fish, he was then told to feed his lambs. He was to preach the gospel. Since the gospel was to go to all nations, the 153 fish are understood as a type of the nations to which the gospel was to go. That there were exactly this number of nations at the time, however, is doubtful.

In his commentary on Ezekiel 47:6-12, Jerome wrote that Greek zoologists had recorded 153 different kinds of fish, thus the 153 fish represented men of all types, or nations, who were to receive the gospel. But the number is not proved. The source quoted by Jerome (as it has come down to us at least) is 157. Pliny spoke of 104 varieties of fish.

Some believe that Christ called not only one group of "seventy" to preach the gospel during his earthly ministry, but two groups of seventy—"seventy other" (Lk. 10:1). If, according to this theory, there were two sets of seventy, this would make 140. Add to this the 12 apostles, plus Jesus Christ, the apostle of our profession (Hebrews 3:1) and we have a total of 153!

Cyril of Alexandria broke the number down as follows: 100 equals the fulness of the Gentiles, 50 the remnant of Israel, and the three, the Father, Son, and Holy Spirit.

Augustine gave a mathematical approach. He pointed out that 153 is the total of all numbers from 1 through 17, then gave various theories regarding the number 17.

Another view is based on the numerical value of the name *Simon*, which is 76, and that of *ichthys*, fish, which is 77. Added together, these numbers total 153.

My personal opinion is that these theories prove nothing one way or the other. While it is not impossible that there was some special meaning regarding the exact number of fish, 153, it is also possible that this verse simply records the number of fish caught by Peter.

JONAH

We have all heard the story of Jonah and his experience with "a great fish." Repeatedly the scriptures use the word "down" in describing his path of disobedience. He was a prophet who lived in Gath-hepher (2 Kings 14:23-25) and was called to go to Nineveh. Nineveh, we know, was the capital of Assyria. The Assyrians were the enemies of Israel. With the extreme religious differences, national differences, and political differences that existed between the two countries, we can understand why Jonah did not want to go to Nineveh. But why—as we are told in the story—in his attempt to flee from the presence of the Lord, did he want to go to *Tarshish?*

I used to wonder about this. Then one day I was reading about King Solomon and the ships he sent to Tarshish. "For the king's ships went to Tarshish with the servants of Huram: every three years came the ships of Tarshish bringing gold, and silver, ivory and apes, and peacocks" (2 Chron. 9:21). The exports for which Tarshish was known were gold, silver, ivory, apes, and peacocks! Granted, we are sermonizing a bit here, but consider these things!

Tarshish was a land of *gold and silver*, a land of riches and wealth. Here, he might become wealthy. How many today have been ruined because they became obsessed with a love for silver and gold! Like the children of Israel, they have danced around a golden calf, worshiping GOLD instead of GOD. Judas betrayed the Lord for thirty pieces of silver. Many examples could be given from the scriptures and history. Many, like Jonah, are fleeing from God's presence for the silver and gold of this world. How much better to be like Peter who said: "Silver and gold have I none," but he had the power to heal the sick beggar in the name of Jesus!

Tarshish was also a land of *ivory*. This might typify luxury. Luxury can be a blessing; but not at the expense of missing God's call! Ivory might be a type of rulership. King Solomon once made a throne of ivory (1 Kings 10:18). In religious circles today, some will shun God's call or compromise to gain a position of leadership. But there is no such thing as a big "I" and a little "u" in God's program.

Tarshish was a land of *apes and peacocks*. The ape could be a type of that which is unclean, counterfeit, and vulgar. The peacock is recognized as a symbol of pride. Pride is not of God. The middle letter in pride is "I". Pride, no doubt, was a definite part of Jonah's downward path.

THE PEACOCK.

Jonah, we notice, did not say he would not go anywhere. No, he would go—but he went the wrong direction. Many today, likewise, reject God's will for their lives and flee, as it were, to a land of silver, gold, ivory, apes, and peacocks! They want Christianity without Christ, a crown without a cross, promises without commandments. They have a form of godliness, but deny the power thereof.

We are told that Jonah went down to Joppa (Jonah 1:3). Peter, centuries later, also went to Joppa. When Peter was there, he stayed with "Simon a tanner, whose house was by the *sea side*" (Acts 10:6). Jonah was also by the sea side in Joppa, for it was here that he boarded a ship. In *location*, then, they may have been very close to the same spot. Everything else, however, is *contrast*.

Jonah went to Joppa to FLEE from God; Peter was in Joppa SEEKING God. The one went DOWN into a boat; the other went UP to the housetop. The one FELL asleep; the other FELL into a trance and received revelations from God. The one REBELLED at a missionary call; the other RECEIVED a missionary call—and that call changed the course of the world!

We have heard people say: "We knew we were in the will of God—everything went smoothly, there were no problems of any kind!" Well, this does not necessarily indicate one is in the will of God. The apostle Paul was in the will of God and yet things did not always go smoothly for him! On the other hand, just because people have trouble does not indicate they are in the will of God, either. In Jonah's case, his trouble was the result of disobedience!

A terrific storm came up at sea. The sailors began to pray to their gods, but to no avail. The shipmaster awakened Jonah and told him to pray to his God. But the storm continued. Then they cast lots [compare the word "lottery"] and the lot fell upon Jonah. With all of his mistakes, yet we can see real character in this man Jonah. He admitted the trouble was his fault and was willing even to lay down his life for others.

The men rowed hard. But it was not until Jonah was thrown overboard that the waters became calm. When this happened, "the men feared the Lord exceedingly, and offered a *sacrifice* unto the Lord" (Jonah 1:16). It is not unusual to read about sacrifices being offered in the Old Testament. But this sacrifice was unique because it is the only sacrifice mentioned in the Bible which was offered on a *boat*!

Now we are told that the Lord had prepared a great fish to swallow Jonah. Underneath *are* the everlasting arms! (We have included here a curious Medieval drawing.) Jonah had quite an

experience, but then so did the fish. I can imagine after the fish "vomited out Jonah upon the dry land" that it headed back to deeper water and said: "Wheeee! if there's anything that makes me sick to my stomach, it's a backslidden preacher! I wonder what denomination he's with?"

This time Jonah obeyed the Lord's commission and went to Nineveh. His message was right to the point: "Forty days", he cried, "and Nineveh shall be overthrown." But what happened? "The people of Nineveh believed God." They began to fast. The king called the city to repentance. And to show God they meant business, they not only put sackcloth on themselves, they even put it on their *animals*. Imagine a goat or dog walking around Nineveh wearing sackcloth! "And God saw their works, that they turned from their evil way; and God repented of the evil, that he had said he would do unto them; and he did it not" (Jonah 3:10).

Then Jonah got his feelings hurt. God had made him look like a false prophet—he felt. "And the Lord God prepared a gourd and made it come up over Jonah, that it might be a shadow over his head, to deliver him from his grief" (Jonah 4:6). Jonah made this plant his tent, its thick branches and large leaves making an ample shelter for him. What kind of plant was this? Not that it makes any difference, but it is generally believed by Biblical scholars that it was the tree from which *castor oil* is obtained.

JOSHUA AND JERICHO

We have all heard of Joshua and the battle of Jericho. But the words of Joshua when the city was destroyed are not so well-known: "Cursed be the man before the Lord, that riseth up and buildeth this city Jericho: he shall lay the foundation thereof in his firstborn, and in his youngest son shall he set up the gates of it" (Joshua 6:26).

Over 500 years later these words found fulfillment in the days of Ahab. "In his days did Hiel the Bethelite build Jericho: he laid the foundation thereof in Abiram his firstborn, and set up the gates thereof in his youngest son Segub, according to the word of the Lord which he spake by Joshua" (1 Kings 16:34).

Some think the words "he shall lay the foundation thereof in his firstborn, and in his youngest son shall he set up the gates of it", were to convey the idea of great delay, that the rebuilding of Jericho would be accompanied with enough problems so that it would take a good portion of one's life. If the foundation would be laid at the time a man's first child was born, his youngest (and last) son would be born before the walls would be completed and ready for gates to be set up to them. This would give the passage a proverbial meaning, showing that all the years the builder would be capable of procreating children—so would he face hindrances and delays in rebuilding Jericho.

Another view is that Hiel may have actually sacrificed his children in the walls, supposing this would guarantee their strength! We cannot say with certainty that this was the case, but some archaeologists hold this view and we do know that this custom was performed at various times and places.

In Japan when a great wall was to be built, a slave would offer himself as a part of the foundation. In Siam when a new city gate was being built, officers would seize several persons and bury them under it as "guardian angels." At one place in Africa a boy and girl used to be buried alive before the great gate of a city to make it secure. In Europe, the Picts are said to have bathed their foundation stones in human blood, especially in building forts or castles. Legend has it that a child was walled into the castle of Liebenstein. Another legend has it that the wall of Copenhagen sank as fast as it was built. So they took an innocent little girl and walled her in. Music was played to hide her screams and the wall was built—and stood fast from then on.

If Hiel held the superstitious belief that walls would be secure because of human sacrifices, we can see why he may have taken drastic measures, especially with the walls of *Jericho*. He no doubt knew the history of how those walls came tumbling down centuries before in the days of Joshua. (We have included an old drawing from the book by Josephus depicting that time.)

ELIJAH—DID HE GO TO HEAVEN?

One day at a location near Jericho (2 Kings 2:15) the prophet Elijah was suddenly taken up from the earth. The Bible does not say it was in a *chariot of fire* that he was taken up. What the Bible actually says it this: "And it came to pass, as they [Elijah and Elisha] went on, and talked, that, behold, there appeared a chariot of fire, and horses of fire, and parted them both asunder; and Elijah went up by a *whirlwind* into heaven" (2 Kings 2:11).

There is some question about the word heaven here. There are *three* heavens mentioned in the Bible (2 Cor. 12:2) which are usually explained in the following manner: the first heaven is the atmosphere, where the birds fly; the second is the stratosphere, where the stars are; the third is the throne of God. We see the first heaven by day, the second by night, and the third by faith. Into *which* heaven was Elijah taken by a whirlwind?

It is commonly believed that Elijah was taken clear up into the third heaven, to the very throne of God. But according to John 3:13, "No man hath ascended up to heaven, but he that came down from heaven"—Jesus Christ himself. On the basis of this verse, some believe that the whirlwind actually took Elijah up into the *atmospheric* heaven and to another location on *earth*.

If we look into the context, we see that the sons of the prophets knew that Elijah was to be taken away (2 Kings 2:3). Elijah said he would be "taken away" from Elisha (verse 9). This had been revealed. But the idea that he would be taken to heaven, as we think of heaven as the throne of God, is not even hinted at. Instead, after he was "taken away", the sons of the prophets went out *looking for him*. They searched for three days, even though Elisha had told them their efforts would be in vain (verses 17, 18).

In support of the belief that Elijah was caught away to another location on earth, is the fact that several years *after* he was taken away, King Jehoram received a letter from him! There are some difficulties in figuring the *exact* chronology involved, but for our present purpose, we will simply say the letter was written and received *after* Elijah's whirlwind experience. Figures on how long after vary from two years to ten or more. A note in *Josephus* says four years, while the *Jewish Encyclopedia* has it figured at seven years.

Regardless of how many years later it was, "there came a writing to him (Jehoram) from Elijah the prophet, saying..." (2 Chron. 21:12). The wickedness of Jehoram (sometimes spelled Joram), for which he was rebuked in the letter, happened *after* Elijah was taken away, yet the letter speaks of these things as *past*, and the judgment to come upon him as *future*. So the idea that Elijah wrote the letter *before* he was taken away, as some believe, seems very improbable.

If, however, Elijah had been caught away to another location on *earth*—even though in God's purpose his whereabouts was unrevealed—this would explain most logically the letter sent to Jehoram. Some copies of *Josephus* come right out and offer this explanation: "For he was yet upon earth" (*Antiquities of the Jews*, 9, 5:2).

If, then, Elijah was still somewhere on earth when he wrote this letter, did he later die? A marginal note (found in some editions of the Bible) concerning Elijah's letter says this: "...which was writ before his death", meaning, evidently, the death of Elijah. There is a traditional site of Elijah's *tomb* near a tributary of the Jordan River. *Harper's Bible Dictionary* (p. 760), which lists various feasts and fasts of the Jewish calendar, says the tenth day of the second month Ziv was a "fast to commemorate the *death* of Elijah."

It should be pointed out, however, that among the Jews there were many who believed the other way. These accepted the idea that Elijah was assumed into heaven or was, as a glorified individual, still present at times on earth. When some thought Jesus, on the cross, had called for Elijah, they said: "Let us see whether Elias [Elijah] will come to save him" (Matt. 27:47-49). It hardly seems they believed Elijah would be *raised from the dead* in order to do this.

When Jesus performed so many miracles, the various opinions which were being expressed were that "John was *risen* from the dead" or that "Elias [Elijah] had *appeared*", or that "one of the old prophets was *risen* again" (Lk. 9:7, 8). The implication is that John (who had been beheaded) and the prophets would have to be *raised from the dead* in order to fit this role. But of Elijah, it was

43

said, he would only have to "appear".

Was Elijah taken by a whirlwind into the heaven of God's throne? Unless we allow for an exception, John 3:13, "No man hath ascended up to heaven, but he that came down from heaven", seems conclusive. It is an interesting subject, but whichever viewpoint we accept regarding Elijah, an element of mystery remains. But if all the details are not known, why should this worry us?

Many things are not explained. Joseph, the husband of Mary, is mentioned during the childhood of Jesus. But he is never mentioned again after Jesus was age 12. We assume he died, for Jesus (when he was dying) asked John to watch after his mother. But the details are not given. We are not told in the scriptures what Jesus did from the time he was 12 until he was about 30 years of age. These are called the 18 silent years. Theories have been written. We can speculate. But the Bible leaves the subject silent. What became of the robe of Christ, we do not know, but this has served as the basis for a novel and a motion picture, *The Robe*. The scriptures do not reveal a date for the second coming of Christ, even though men have repeatedly attempted to establish dates for this event. God not only *reveals*, he also *conceals* things. This is his business. He has told us enough!

* * * * *

A young theologian named Fiddle,
Refused to accept his degree,
'Tis bad enough being named Fiddle,
Without being Fiddle D. D.

44

Chapter 4

DEATH, BURIAL, AND RESURRECTION

We have often heard people say something like this: "We need to lift up Jesus. Jesus said that if we lift him up, he will draw all men unto him." They mean well by saying such things—to be sure. But when Jesus spoke about being lifted up, he was speaking of his *death*—that he would be killed by *crucifixion*! Here is the passage:

"And I, if I be lifted up from the earth, will draw all men unto me. THIS HE SAID, SIGNIFYING WHAT DEATH HE SHOULD DIE" (John 12:32, 33).

Jesus would not die from sickness. He would not die from old age. He would not die from being stoned or thrown over a cliff. He would not die by being drowned at sea. He would die by being lifted up—by crucifixion. The significance of this amazing prediction of Jesus is not realized when it is misapplied to the preaching of the gospel.

Pilate told the Jews to take Jesus and judge him according to their law. But, being under Roman rule, they said: "It is not lawful for *us* to put any man to death"—which would have probably been by stoning (cf. Acts 7:59)—"that the saying of Jesus might be fulfilled, which he spake, signifying what death he should die" (John 18:31, 32)—referring back to his statement about being lifted up, that is, his death by crucifixion.

TEN THOUSAND ANGELS?

A beautiful hymn about Jesus says, "He could have called ten thousand angels..." It is true that Jesus could have called 10,000 angels to deliver him from being crucified. He could have called 100,000 angels. But what the scripture actually says is this: "...thinkest thou that I cannot now pray to my Father, and he shall presently give me more than *twelve legions* of angels" (Mt. 26:53).

Though the word legion was used to designate different numbers at different times, most often a legion designated 6,000 men. At this rate, twelve legions would have been 72,000. In the immediate context, Peter had drawn out his sword and cut a man's ear off, supposedly to defend Jesus. Perhaps the reason Jesus used the number 12 was as a comparison to the 12 apostles. If he needed help, he had more than just twelve *apostles* to rely on. He could actually call for twelve *legions of angels!*

DID JESUS FALL BENEATH THE CROSS?

It is commonly assumed that Jesus carried his cross part way to Calvary and fell beneath its weight. At this point, someone else was called upon to carry it the rest of the way. But the Bible does *not* say he fell beneath his cross. In fact, it is possible that Jesus never carried the cross at all!

The accounts given by Matthew, Mark, and Luke all tell us it was *Simon the Cyrenian* who carried the cross. There is no mention of *Jesus* carrying it in these gospels. Luke's account says: "And as they led him [Jesus] away"—from where he had been judged by Pilate—"they laid hold upon one *Simon*, a Cyrenian, coming out of the country, and on him they laid the cross, that he might bear it after Jesus" (Lk. 23:26; see also Matt. 27:32; Mk. 15:21).

We should get this picture clearly in focus. "As" they led Jesus away, Simon, a Cyrenian, was compelled to carry the cross. He followed "after" Jesus. We are not told that Jesus carried the cross part way, then Simon picked it up and went on from there.

John's account, if taken alone, seems to imply that it was Jesus who carried the cross—carried it *all the way* to where he was crucified. "And they took Jesus, and led him away. And he bearing his cross went forth into a place called the place of a skull...where they crucified him" (John 19:16-18). The careful reader will notice, however, that the only difference in John's account is that he simply does not state *who* it was that "bearing the cross went forth into a place called the place of a skull." John states that they led Jesus away. Then he says: "And he (whoever it was) bearing his cross (the cross on which Jesus was crucified) went forth into a place called the place of a skull."

According to Luke's account, and also John's, it was when "they led Jesus away" that the cross was placed on the one who carried it to the place of crucifixion. When it is all studied out, there is no room left for the idea that *two* different people carried the cross—Jesus part way and then Simon the rest of the way.

Because of these things, some believe (and I think with good reason) that the word "he" in John's account could be understood as a reference to Simon the Cyrenian. Then there is harmony in all of the accounts. It is not our purpose to be unduly dogmatic on this point. But we can state here quite emphatically this much: the Bible never says Jesus fell beneath his cross. This is only a tradition.

A preacher I know has a little theory that Simon (who carried the cross to Calvary) was the father of the apostle Paul. We are told in Mark 15:21 that Simon the Cyrenian was "the father of Rufus." When Paul wrote to the Christians at Rome, he said: "Salute Rufus chosen in the Lord, and his mother and mine." (Rom. 16:13). By *assuming* that Paul meant this woman was his mother in the *literal* sense, and *assuming* that this Rufus in Rome was the *same* Rufus whose father was from Cyrene, it could be concluded that Simon the Cyrenian was the father (or step-father) of Paul. But we feel the evidence is far from sufficient to warrant this view.

CALVARY—A HILL?

We sing the beautiful hymn, "On a hill far away stood an old rugged cross..." But the Bible does not say Jesus was crucified on a *hill*. The Bible nowhere speaks of a "mount" Calvary or gives the idea that the cross was carried up a road to a mountain top! Instead, we are simply told that Jesus was led to a "place" called Golgotha or Calvary, meaning "the place of a skull" and was crucified (Mt. 27: 33; Mk. 15:22; Lk. 23:33; John 19:17).

There are different theories as to what is meant by the term "the place of a skull." A very old belief is that it was because it was a place of execution and there may have been actual skulls there. A more recent belief is the idea about a *hill*— and that this hill was called Calvary because it had the *appearance* of a skull. This is possible, but it is certainly not conclusive. As *Harper's Bible Dictionary* (p. 87) says: "There is little to substantiate the view of those who accept the skull-like hillock called 'Gordon's Calvary', with its eye-socketed caves recognized in 1849 by Otto Thenius."

Some of us have seen pictures of Gordon's Calvary since childhood. But usually the pictures don't show the noisy bus station with many old busses coming and going right in front of this rocky bluff. I purposely included this when I took this picture on April 7, 1978.

The reason this hill is called *Gordon's* Calvary is because General Gordon, a British soldier, was quite successful in promoting the belief regarding this site. This was in 1882. What about all the centuries before? Does the exposure of this hill as we know it today even reach back to the time of Christ? Rocky bluffs are common to the whole area around Jerusalem. It is not as though this hill has been identified as Calvary for centuries.

Another site which is shown as Calvary was designated by Helena during her visit to Jerusalem in the fourth century. Inside the present tottering structure built over the spot (shared by six Christian groups), the little hillock called "Calvary" is 14 feet high, rising to balcony level. The objection to this site is that it is inside the present north wall of old Jerusalem and we know that Jesus was crucified *outside* the city wall (Heb. 13:12). But, again, we cannot be certain just where the city wall may have been at this point 2,000 years ago.

But does it really matter where the exact site of Calvary was located? The true significance is not where the cross was, what shape the cross was, or who did or didn't carry the cross. The thing that really matters is what was accomplished on that cross at the place called Calvary. "The preaching of the cross is to them that perish foolishness; but unto us which are saved it is the power of God" (1 Cor. 1:18).

WHAT KIND OF GARDEN?

After Jesus was crucified, he was buried in a tomb located in a garden which was nearby (John 19:41). It is not uncommon for us to think of this garden as a beautiful little park-like garden with flowers and roses. We have probably gotten this idea from the hymn which says: "I come to the garden alone, while the dew is still on the *roses*...." But was it a rose garden?

Tertullian of Carthage at the end of the second century spoke of this garden as producing "lettuces" (*De Spectaculis*, xxx). Another second century work, *The Book of the Resurrection*, a Coptic manuscript from Egypt (now in the British Museum) states that the gardener's name was Philogenes whose son Jesus had healed. He spoke of it as "my vegetable garden." The *Epistola contra Judaeos* of Amulo, Archbishop of Lyons, in the ninth century quotes a Jewish tradition that had been handed down that the tomb was "in a garden full of cabbages." It would be useless to argue one of these viewpoints against the others. The Bible doesn't actually say what kind of garden it was. But a gardener worked there (John 20:15) and it was no doubt a garden with some type of crop, not merely a flower garden.

The Church of the Holy Sepulcher, as the name implies, is supposedly built over the tomb in which Jesus was placed.

has favored this site for centuries. (See accompanying photo.) But the idea of "holy spots" can easily lead to superstitious ideas that actually detract from the truth of God, as during the middle ages when some were taught that a visit to this spot was even efficacious to wash away sins!

Another possible location for the tomb is only a short distance from the viewpoint for Gordon's Calvary. This is called the Garden Tomb. It was first discovered in 1867 and was excavated in 1891. It is not a case of this site being visited century after century as we might have supposed. There are actually hundreds of tombs in the area.

According to the scriptures, the tomb of Joseph of Arimathea (in which Jesus was placed) was in a garden, the disciples could look into it from the outside, and there was standing room for a number of persons within the tomb. There is nothing about the Garden Tomb that would conflict with these things. However, going inside the tomb I noticed it is actually a *double* tomb. There are places cut out in the rock for *two* bodies. A rich man, it is explained, might have had a tomb for himself and his wife. But the Bible simply says that Joseph placed the body of Jesus "in *his* own new tomb, which he had hewn out in the rock" (Mt. 27:60). There is no mention of it being a tomb for two.

Was the Garden Tomb the place in which Jesus was buried? We don't know. Interestingly enough, those in charge of the Garden

similar to this. When I was there, those in charge did not encourage people to regard this as a "holy spot", whatever that
might mean. Emphasis was placed rather on the fact that the
tomb—*wherever it might have been*—is an EMPTY tomb! A talk
was given here about the *living* Christ and that he is not in a
tomb, but standing at our heart's door, as it were, willing to come
inside and fill our lives with his presence and power! What a
refreshing contrast to some of the sites one visits on a Holy Land
tour!

THE ASCENSION—FROM WHERE?

Following the ascension of Christ into heaven, we are told that the disciples returned "unto Jerusalem from *the mount called Olivet*, which is from Jerusalem a sabbath day's journey" (Acts 1:12). The mention of the Mount of Olives has caused some to assume that Jesus ascended from this mount—perhaps from the *top* of it. But why the top? Since he had a long distance to go, did he need the summit as a launching pad? The top of the mount, as we shall see, was not the place from which Jesus ascended.

Others think the ascension took place from the spot over which the Church of the Ascension is built. This is on the western slope of the hill, a spot designated by Helena almost 300 years after the ascension took place. The story is that Helena, being very elderly, when climbing up the hill became too tired to go further, so simply gave instructions to build the shrine at that point.

But according to the Bible itself, the ascension was not from the top of the mount or from the area of the Church of the Ascension. Instead, the ascension is linked with Bethany! It is clearly stated. "And he led them out as far as to BETHANY, and he lifted up his hands, and blessed them. And it came to pass, while he blessed them, he was parted from them, and carried up into heaven" (Lk. 24:50, 51). This does not conflict with the statement that they returned to Jerusalem "from the mount called Olivet", for Bethany was located on the southeastern portion of this hill area.

The trip back to Jerusalem, we are told, was a sabbath day's journey (Acts 1:12). This was figured at seven and a half furlongs (or about *one* mile). But in John 11:18, we are told that from Bethany to Jerusalem was about fifteen furlongs (or about *two* miles), which would have been *more* than a sabbath day's journey. At first glance, this presents a difficulty.

But Lightfoot, the noted Biblical scholar, explains: "Our Savior led out his disciples, when he was about to ascend, to the very first region or tract of mount Olivet, which was called Bethany, and was distant from the city a Sabbath day's journey. And so far from the city itself did that tract extend itself which was called Bethphage; and when he was come to that place where the *bound of Bethphage and Bethany met* and touched one

52

another, he then ascended; in that very place where he got upon the ass when he rode into Jerusalem (Mk. 11:1)" (*Clarke's Commentary*, Vol. 5, p. 504).

In view of the distances involved and the information given to us, it appears that when Jesus led his disciples out "*to* Bethany", he did not lead them *into* Bethany, not into the town itself, but rather to the town limit. That the ascension did not take place right in the middle of town seems evident, for after his resurrection he appeared only to certain ones: "...*not to all the people, but unto witnesses chosen before of God*" (Acts 10:41). He was plainly visible when he ascended, but it was not right in the middle of town nor on the western side of the mount of Olives in full view of the city of Jerusalem.

THE UPPER ROOM

After Jesus ascended to heaven, the disciples returned to Jerusalem. "And when they were come in, they went up into an *upper room*, where *abode* both Peter, and James, and Simon Zelotes, and Judas the brother of James" (Acts 1:13).

The next verse says: "These all continued with one accord in prayer and supplication, with the women, and Mary the mother of Jesus, and with the brethren." From these verses we learn that the upper room was where certain of the disciples lived and these (along with others) all continued in one accord in prayer. But WHERE they met for worship and prayer is not explained—not in these verses. But, turning to the book of Luke, we find that the place where they assembled for worship was the *temple*. After the ascension, the disciples "returned to Jerusalem with great joy: and were *continually* in the TEMPLE, praising and blessing God" (Lk. 24:50-53).

On the day of Pentecost when they were all assembled together in one place, there is every reason to believe it was in the temple—not in a comparatively small upper room of a house. Let us carefully notice the following scriptures and see if this is not definitely implied:

Luke 24:52, 53 tells us they were "*continually* in the TEMPLE, praising God..."

Acts 1:14 says: "These all *continued* with *one accord* in prayer."

Acts 2:1 says: "They were all with *one accord* in one place..." (on the day of Pentecost.)

Acts 2:46 says: "And they, *continuing* daily with *one accord* in the TEMPLE ... praising God..."

According to these verses, *before* the day of Pentecost they met in the temple. *After* Pentecost, we are told that the disciples *continued* to meet in the temple. This wording definitely implies they were in the temple on the day of Pentecost. The sound from heaven of a rushing mighty wind "filled all the *house* where they were sitting" (Acts 2:2). The use of the word "house" would not prove they were all in a house in the sense of an individual home. While the Greek word used here (*Strong's Concordance*, –3624) is a general term which can be used of a person's house, it is also used in the expression "house of God"—the temple area where merchandise was sold

(Mk. 1:17) and the same word is translated "temple" in Luke 11:51.

It should be remembered that though the Jews were divided into different groups—groups that were often antagonistic to one another—yet, the temple was a gathering place for them all, regardless of which Jewish sect they belonged to. From the scriptures and other records, we know that the temple had vast corridors or "porches" which served as regular meeting places for the various groups.

Special mention is made in the Bible of one of these sections called "Solomon's Porch" in which there were benches so that large crowds could be addressed. It was in this section of the temple that a crowd gathered to hear Peter preach after the healing of the lame man. Peter and John were on their way up to the *temple* to pray when the man was healed, and "he leaping up stood, and walked, and entered with them into the temple . . . and all the people ran together unto them in the *porch that is called Solomon's* greatly wondering" (Acts 3:8, 11). This area became the regular meeting place for those who were followers of Jesus Christ. "And they were all with one accord in *Solomon's Porch* and . . . believers were the more added to the Lord" (Acts 5:12).

The fact that 3,000 were converted from Peter's preaching on the day of Pentecost, shows that the crowd was very large. An "upper room" of that period which served as living quarters for some preachers would hardly be large enough to admit that many people! But with the belief that these things took place within a section of the temple, there is no problem for space. It has been estimated that the vast temple area was capable of holding 210,000 people.

ONE HUNDRED AND TWENTY?

How many followers of Jesus received the Holy Spirit in the initial outpouring of the Spirit on Pentecost? It is commonly believed there were "one hundred and twenty". But when the Bible mentions 120 disciples, it was actually not in connection with the day of Pentecost, but on a day when one was chosen to replace Judas.

Turning to Acts 1:15 we read: "And in those days (between the ascension and Pentecost) Peter stood up in the midst of the disciples, and said, (the number of names together were about an hundred and twenty) . . ." The Phillips translation says: "It was during this period that Peter stood up among the brothers—there were about a hundred and twenty present AT THE TIME—and said . . ."

One hundred and twenty was the number of men that the Jews required to form a council in a city, so this number of disciples being present was apparently considered enough to go ahead and appoint a man to replace Judas. But this cannot prove that 120 was the sum total of all the believers at that time.

Turning to First Corinthians 15:6, we read that Jesus appeared to "FIVE HUNDRED brethren" on one occasion after his resurrection. These to whom the Lord appeared were commissioned to receive the Holy Spirit. Are we to believe that all of these except 120 "backslid" and, consequently, did not receive the Spirit? Are we to believe that these who actually saw the resurrected Christ did not remain faithful even for a few days until Pentecost? No, surely there was more reality in seeing the resurrected Christ than this!

Even years later, when Paul wrote his epistle to the Corinthians, he still spoke of these 500 disciples as "brethren." Some, by then, had died, but many of them were still alive and were still called brethren. They had not lost out with God.

Taking all of these things into consideration, it is far from conclusive to teach that there were only 120 that received the Holy Spirit on the day of Pentecost. The 120 are mentioned in Acts ONE; whereas, in Acts TWO the implication is that not just a limited number of the believers was present, but that "ALL" followers of Christ were there in one accord and were filled with the Spirit.

Some, believing the disciples were in the upper room at Pentecost, think a special blessing awaits them when they visit this room on a tour to the holy land. But if what we have said is correct, the disciples were *not even in the upper room* when the Spirit was poured out at Pentecost!

Besides, the upper room that is shown in Jerusalem dates back only to the *eleventh century* and was built by the crusaders! No building in Jerusalem today dates back to the time of Jesus, for as Jesus himself predicted, such destruction would come upon that city that one stone would not be left upon another (Luke 19:41-44). These words found fulfillment in 70 A.D. when the Roman armies destroyed the city.

HOLY LAND TOURS

In view of the fact that the Jerusalem which stood at the time of Jesus was destroyed and the uncertainty that exists regarding many of the sacred sites, I have sometimes been asked if I recommend a tour to the land of the Bible. I will say this, if you can, if you enjoy travel, if you have the desire, why not? It is different than a trip to any other land because it was here that so many events in the Bible happened.

While we may not know today the *exact* spots where certain events took place, we can recognize general areas with certainty. The Dead Sea, into which the Jordan river flows, is easily identified. It is the *lowest spot on earth*, 1,300 feet below sea level! When I was there, our guide told a story about three boys who were bragging about what their fathers had done. One was from New York, one was from Paris, and one from Israel. The one from New York said: "You know the Empire State Building, my father *built* that." The boy from Paris said: "You know the Eiffel tower, my father *built* that." The boy from Israel said: "You know the Dead Sea, my father *killed* that!"

There can be little doubt about the location of the Mount of Olives, the old Temple site, or of the city of Jerusalem. No doubt the stones in some of the old walls and buildings are stones that were used in ancient buildings, for the city has been destroyed and rebuilt several times. A trip to Jerusalem is a unique experience and the land *is* the land in which Jesus lived.

Those who cannot make such a trip, however, need not feel left out. We are just as close to God wherever we are. God has poured out his Spirit upon all flesh and we need not go to Jerusalem to find Him! "Believe me," Jesus said, "the hour cometh, when ye shall neither in this mountain, nor yet at Jerusalem, worship the Father...The hour cometh, and *now* is, when the true worshippers shall worship the Father in spirit and in truth: for the Father seeketh such to worship him" (John 4:21-23).

Chapter 5

UNUSUAL NAMES OF THE BIBLE

According to the Bible, NOAH was a woman.

I have sometimes gotten the attention of an audience by announcing, among other things, that my message would prove this point. The Noah of ark-and-flood fame was, of course, a man. Not as well-known as this Noah was the *woman* by this name. Zelophehad had five daughters, but no sons. When he died, the question of inheritance came up. Normally an inheritance was passed on to the sons of a family, but since he had no sons, the inheritance was given to his daughters, one of which was Noah. It is all explained in Numbers 27:1-7.

Many might think of GOMER as a man's name, which indeed it was (Gen. 10:2). But it was also a *woman's* name in the Bible. Gomer was the wife of the prophet Hosea (Hosea 1:3). The name NUN causes us to think of a woman, one belonging to a religious order. But Nun was a *man*, the father of Joshua (Ex. 33:11). A *boy* named HEN seems strange. It is like the boy named "Sue" in a popular Johnny Cash song a few years ago. Hen, meaning favor or grace, was the son of Zephaniah who is mentioned in Zechariah (6:14).

Men's names outnumber women's names about 17 to 1 in the Bible. The names of men were commonly given in family trees. Today, it is a custom for a woman to take the name (last name) of her husband at marriage, while her maiden name may become comparatively obscure.

The Bible mentions a man named HEMAN. (I wonder if he was a he-man?) "And God gave to Heman fourteen sons and three daughters. All these were under the hands of their father for song in the house of the Lord, with cymbals, psalteries, and harps" (1 Chron. 25:5, 6).

Names like HOD (1 Chron. 7:37), BUNNI (Neh. 11:15), MASH (Gen. 10:23), NON (1 Chron. 8:12), HUZ and BUZ (Gen. 22:20, 21) are quite different.

There is also the case of BEDAD who was HADAD'S dad. Or

to put it another way, Hadad had a dad named Bedad (Gen. 36:35). This is only a play on words and not nearly as strange as the case of two women who were the mothers of their half-brothers and whose father was their children's grandfather (Gen. 19:30-38).

Three different men in the Bible were named DODO. There was Dodo, a man of Issachar (Judges 10:1), Dodo the Alohite (2 Sam. 23:9), and Dodo of Bethlehem (2 Sam. 23:24).

The Bible mentions a king of Egypt named SO (2 Kings 17:4). Someone might ask: "Is that So?", and the reply: "Yes, that's So." There was a large city in Egypt named NO (Ezekiel 30:14-16), but I don't know if So ever went to No. In addition to a city named No, Egypt also had a city named ON (Gen. 41:45).

AI, a town about 12 miles north of Jericho, holds the distinction of being the only city or town mentioned in the Bible which has to be *spelled* in order to be *pronounced* (Joshua 7:2).

We all know of Adam, the first man. But there was also a *city* named ADAM (Joshua 3:16). Tarshish, the land to which Jonah sought to flee, is best known as a *place*. But there was also a man named TARSHISH (Gen. 10:4). Some names of cities or towns in the United States (which were also names of places mentioned in the Bible) are as follows:

ABILENE, Texas (Lk. 3:1).

ANTIOCH, California (Acts 11:26).

ATHENS, Georgia (Acts 17:22).

BABYLON, New York (Matt. 1:11).

BETHANY, Missouri (Matt. 21:17).

BETHEL, Connecticut (Gen. 12:8)

BETHLEHEM, Pennsylvania (Matt. 2:1).

CARMEL, California (1 Sam. 25:2).

CYPRUS, California (Acts 11:19).

DOTHAN, Alabama (2 Kings 6:13).

EPHRAIM, Utah (John 11:54).

GOSHEN, California (Gen. 45:10).

LEBANON, Oregon (Deut. 1:7).

MOAB, Utah (Num. 21:11).

MEMPHIS, Tennessee (Hosea 9:6).

PALESTINE, Texas (Joel 3:4).

PARADISE, California (2 Cor. 12:4).

PHILADELPHIA, Pennsylvania (Rev. 3:7).

ROME, Georgia (Rom. 1:7).

SALEM, Oregon (Heb. 7:1).

SARDIS, Mississippi (Rev. 3:1).

SELAH, Washington (2 Kings 14:7).

SYRACUSE, New York (Acts 28:12).

ZION, Illinois (Joel 2:1).

I have purposely left out of this list some very tiny places in the United States with names such as Eden, Jerusalem, Hell, etc.

In one church a teacher was speaking about the distance from Dan to Beersheba (1 Sam. 3:20). One member of the class inquired: "Do I understand that Dan and Beersheba are the names of *places*?"

"Yes."

"Oh", said the inquirer, "I always thought they were husband and wife, like Sodom and Gomorrah"!

The names of men like Joseph, Gideon, Solomon and Joshua are well-known. Not so well-known are the other names by which they were called. Joseph (son of Jacob) was called ZAPHNATH-PAANEAH (Gen. 41:45). Gideon was called JERUBBAAL (Judges 8:35). Solomon was called JEDIDIAH (2 Sam. 12:25). Joshua's original name was HOSEA (Num. 13:16, 11:28).

We know the three Hebrew children who were thrown into the furnace of fire by the names Shadrach, Meshach, and Abednego. But these were not their original names. You see, the king of Babylon had conquered Judah. Young men such as these (and also Daniel) were castrated, made into *eunuchs* to serve as slaves in the king's palace. Isaiah had prophesied that the people of Judah would be "carried to Babylon...and thy sons shall they take away; and they shall be *eunuchs* in the palace of the king of Babylon" (Isaiah 39:6, 7). It was in just this capacity that Daniel, Shadrach, Meshach, and Abednego were made to serve.

NAMES HAD MEANINGS

The original names of the three Hebrew children were Hananiah, Mishael, and Azariah. It was as eunuch-slaves they were renamed Shadrach, Meshach, and Abednego by the prince in charge of the eunuchs (Daniel 1:6, 7). Names in the Bible commonly had meanings. The name Daniel [God is my judge] was changed in Babylon to Belteshatstsar, "The treasure of Bel." Hananiah [The Lord has been gracious to me] was changed to Shadrach, "The inspiration of the sun." Mishael [He who comes from God] was changed to Meshach, "He who belongs to the goddess Sheshach" (a Babylonian deity mentioned in Jeremiah 25:26). Azariah [The Lord is my helper] was changed to Abednego, "The servant of Nego" (a Babylonian god). The degradation of being made eunuch-slaves and given these names is apparent.

We know the meaning of the name Jesus is "savior." This is explained in verses like Matthew 1:21: "...and thou shalt call his name JESUS: *for* he shall *save* his people from their sins." Not only is he the savior, he is the *only* savior. "Neither is there salvation in any other: for there is none other name under heaven given among men, whereby we must be saved" (Acts 4:12).

He has been given a name above every name. The *first* verse in the New Testament begins by mentioning Jesus Christ. The *last*

 verse in the Bible mentions Jesus Christ. He is at the first and also the last; he is called "alpha" and "omega," (the first and last letter of the Greek alphabet as seen in the illustration) the beginning and the ending (Rev. 1:8). Almost every book of the New Testament mentions Jesus in its very first verse.

The disciples preached in his name, baptized in his name, healed the sick in his name, signs followed in his name, prayer was offered in his name. They believed, in fact, in doing all things in his name (Col. 3:17).

The name Jesus is mentioned almost *one thousand* times in the Bible. It always refers to Jesus Christ, except in a few places in which the name is applied to others. Joshua, the son of Nun, is called Jesus in Acts 7:45 and Hebrews 4:8. The name Jose (in the King James Version) is, in some translations, Jesus (Lk. 3:29). Also there was a Jesus called Justus mentioned in Colossians 4:11 and a sorcerer, a false prophet, named Bar-jesus (Acts 13:6).

The names Job gave to his daughters had distinct meanings. One was Kezia or Cassia, a highly cherished and fragrant spice of antiquity. One was named Keren-huppuch, meaning "horn of eye paint," a name linked with the custom of marking a dark color around the eyes. And one was called Jemima, meaning "fair as the day" or a "dove." Later, when her sister gave birth to a baby, she could have been properly called *Aunt* Jemima!

There is a point that is sometimes overlooked regarding the name of the runaway slave Onesimus. His name has the meaning of "useful" or "profitable." Realizing this, we can see there was a play on words in the letter of Paul to Philemon—a point that has commonly gone unnoticed. "I beseech thee for my son Onesimus [profitable], whom I have begotten in my bonds: which in time past was to thee unprofitable [just the opposite of what his name means!], but now profitable [as his name means!] to thee and to me..." (Philemon 10, 11). The runaway slave, having been converted and returning to Philemon, could now truly live up to his name.

When Paul wrote the letter to Philemon, he referred to himself as "Paul the *aged*" (verse 9). It is not uncommon for people to think of Paul as an *old* man. Of course he grew old. However, at the time of his converstion he was a *young* man, growing old only after many years of very fruitful ministry. He is plainly spoken of as a young man in Acts 7:58. Those who stoned Stephen laid their garments "at a *young* man's feet, whose name was Saul [Paul]". Shortly after this he was converted (Acts 9).

Saul was but another name of Paul (Acts 13:9). He probably had both names from the first, one being Hebrew, the other Roman. At the first of his ministry (as recorded in Acts) he is called Saul, but later as his ministry began to spread through many parts of the empire, the Roman name Paul fitly became prominent.

Probably the *strangest* name in the Bible—also the *longest* name in the Bible—is the eighteen-letter name of Isaiah's son MAHERSHALALHASHBAZ! It also has a distinct meaning. "Then said the Lord to me, Call his name Mahershalalhasbaz [Make haste to the spoil; fall upon the prey]. For before the child shall have knowledge to cry, My father and my mother, the riches of Damascus and the spoil of Samaria shall be taken away before the king of Assyria" (Isaiah 8:3, 4).

This symbolic name given to the child indicated that within a short time the king of Assyria would conquer Damascus and Samaria. The prophecy found its fulfillment within three years when Tiglath-pileser, king of Assyria, took Damascus and carried the people captive to Kir. He also took the Reubenites, the Gadites, and the half-tribe of Manasseh as captives into Assyria (2 Kings 15:29, 16:9, 1 Chron. 5:26).

Without first *and* last names (as now), we can see how common names could be easily mistaken for different people. I know one preacher who believes Judas Iscariot was the *brother* of Jesus; that is, that Mary was the mother of them both: "...is not his mother called Mary? and his brethren, James, and Joses, and Simon, and JUDAS" (Matt. 13:55). Actually, though, Judas was a common name at the time; there is no reason to believe that *this* Judas was Judas Iscariot.

Others have worked out a theory that Judas Iscariot was the son of the apostle Peter. Have you heard this? I had not been in the ministry too long (it was the year 1958) when a woman—quite

63

enthusiastically—presented this view to me. She explained that this was why Peter became so upset on the night of our Lord's betrayal—because *his own son* was the one that betrayed Christ! But was Judas the son of Simon Peter?

Consider the following passages: "Then Simon Peter answered...we believe and are sure that thou art the Christ... Jesus answered them, Have not I chosen you twelve, and one of you is a devil? He spake of Judas Iscariot *the son of Simon*" (John 6:68-71). "...Judas Iscariot, *Simon's son*, which should betray him" (John 12:4). "...Judas Iscariot, *Simon's son*" (John 13:2). "And when he had dipped the sop, he gave it to Judas Iscariot, the *son of Simon*" (John 13:26). The expression "son of Simon" is mentioned without explanation, which would probably indicate that the Simon referred to was known to the company of apostles. But, still, this would not prove that Judas was the son of Simon Peter, the apostle. There were a number of men by the name of Simon in the Bible: two apostles (Matt. 10:2-4), Simon of Nazareth (Matt. 13:55), Simon the leper (Matt. 26:6), Simon of Cyrene (Matt. 27:32), Simon the Pharisee (Lk. 7: 40-44), Simon the sorcerer (Acts 6:9), and Simon the tanner of Joppa (Acts 10:6). Being a common name at that time, the statement that Judas was the son of Simon could have referred to any number of men. Most translations do not include the phrase "son of Simon" in the passages we have quoted from the King James Version.

LETTERS OF THE ALPHABET

You won't find the name Woodrow in the Bible—or Wilson—or any other name beginning with the letter "W." The reason for this is because there was no corresponding Hebrew letter with this sound to be used in proper names. Most other letters of the alphabet are represented in Biblical names, however, as the following shows:

A—Adam, B—Benjamin, C—Cain, D—David, E—Elijah, F—Festus, G—Gideon, H—Hosea, I—Isaac, J—Jacob, K—Keturah, L—Lot, M—Mary, N—Nicodemus, O—Obadiah, P—Paul, Q—Quartus, R—Ruth, S—Sarah, T—Timothy, U—Uriah, V—Vashti. W, X, and Y are exceptions, but not Z!

We do not commonly use names which begin with Z. But in the

Bible there are 87 different personal names beginning with the letter "Z", representing 188 individuals! There are 27 Zechariahs, 12 Zichris, 9 Zebadiahs, 9 Zodoks, 7 Zabads, 7 Zaccurs, 7 Zerahs, and 5 Zedekiahs. One of the sons of Jonathan was named Zaza (1 Chron. 2:33).

"The quick red fox jumps over the lazy brown dog." This sentence is sometimes used when one is learning to type or testing the various keys on a typewriter because it includes *all* the letters of the alphabet. In the Bible, Ezra 7:21 uses all the letters of the alphabet, *except one*. "And I, even I Artaxerxes the king, do make a decree to all the treasurers which are beyond the river, that whatsoever Ezra the priest, the scribe of the law of the God of heaven, shall require of you, it be done speedily."

The one letter not found in this verse is the letter "j." However, the letter "j" in English is but a variant of the letter "i." Notice that a "j" is actually an "i" only with the bottom portion curved. In the original King James Version each letter was printed the same, as in Luke 11:6: "For a friend of mine in his iourney is come to me . . ." (see page 74). Alexander Cruden's *Concordance of the Bible* (as printed in 1737), lists words beginning with "i" and "j" under "i" as if they were the same letter. The distinction between these letters was not entirely made until the nineteenth century. Prior to this, then, Ezra 7:21 held the distinction of containing *all* letters of the alphabet.

Several verses have all letters except the letter "q." "Now I Nebuchadnezzar praise and extol and honour the King of heaven, all whose works are truth, and his ways judgment: and those that walk in pride he is able to abase" (Dan. 4:37; also Joshua 7:24, 1 Kings 1:9, 2 Chron. 36:10, Ezekiel 28:13, Hag. 1:1).

Two verses include all letters except the letter "z" (2 Kings 16:15; 1 Chron. 4:10). In the *New* Testament, Galatians 1:14 contains all letters but "k." "And profited in the Jews' religion above many my equals in mine own nation, being more exceedingly zealous of the traditions of my fathers."

BIBLICAL FACTS

God is not specifically mentioned in the Song of Solomon, though some feel the book refers to God allegorically. It has been said that the book of Esther does not mention *or* refer to God.

This is true according to the Hebrew text as it now stands and translations based on it. But the Septuagint version (which was commonly quoted by the New Testament writers) does include the word "God" in Esther 2:20. After the words, "Esther had not yet showed her kindred", the Septuagint version says: "For so Mordecai had charged her to fear GOD, and to keep his commandments, as she did when with him." All other books of the Bible unmistakably mention God.

Various estimates are given as to the time required to read the Bible through. Each person can easily determine how long it would take him to read the Bible by the following method: read one page and note the time, then multiply this by the number of pages in whatever printed edition he may be using. The Bible I have before me now has 339 pages in the New Testament. Figuring two minutes to a page, this would be about 11 hours of reading. Having determined his own time, a person can figure out how many minutes out of the 1,440 minutes we are given each day that he may want to set aside for Bible reading.

Many of us take owning a personal copy of the Bible for granted. But before the invention of the printing press, Bibles had to be hand copied—a task which took even an industrous scribe *at least a year* to complete. How many of us could afford a Bible if it cost a year's salary? Bibles are now available at prices almost everyone can afford and there are even organizations which give *free* copies.

The Bible comes in various shapes, sizes, and colors. It is available on records and tapes. It has been put on tiny micro-film, while some Bibles are quite large. The largest Bible I have ever heard of is the one which was hand printed by a man and his daughter in Los Angeles, California. It weighs 1,094 pounds and is 8 feet high! Another unique Bible is one in the library of the University of Gottingen which is written on 2,470 palm leaves.

The words "his mercy endureth for ever" appear 26 times in one chapter of the Bible—in *every single verse* of Psalm 136. Exodus, chapter 26, has 20 verses having the first three words alike: "And thou shalt..." Numbers, chapter 33, has 42 verses which have the first two words alike: "And they..." Numbers, chapter 7, is unique because the statements of 4 verses are repeated 12 times in this one chapter. This same chapter also speaks of the Israelites using six "covered wagons." This expression causes most of us to think of pioneer days when settlers journeyed west in this country. But covered wagons are mentioned clear back in Numbers 7:3.

The book of Psalms is the *middle* book of the Bible and also the *longest* book. It has 43,743 words. The *shortest* book is Third John with 299 words. The longest verse in the Bible is Esther 8:9 which has 90 words. The *shortest* verse is John 11:35, "Jesus wept." The verb used here signifies the *silent* shedding of tears and is not used anywhere else in the New Testament. It stands in contrast to the audible weeping of the Jews mentioned in verses 31, 33.

The *shortest* chapter in the Bible is Psalm 117 which is a chapter of praise. "O praise the Lord, all ye nations: praise him, all ye people. For his merciful kindness is great toward us: and the truth of the Lord endureth for ever. Praise ye the Lord." Interestingly enough, Psalm 117 is not only the *shortest* chapter in the Bible, it is also the *middle* chapter of the Bible, having 594 chapters before and 594 chapters after it.

*   *   *   *   *

All one has to do to make a mountain out of a molehill is add enough dirt to it. More people are run down by gossip than are run down by automobiles. The tongue is in a wet place, we should watch that it doesn't slip!

*   *   *   *   *

Some people have never learned to give to God. At offering time they get out a little coin and squeeze it so tight that poor old Abe Lincoln would think the Civil War was on again. A little tear comes out and runs down their face. As they look at the coin, they inwardly sing: "When we part I cannot grin, God be with you 'till we meet again." But God loves a *cheerful* giver! (2 Cor. 9:7).

Chapter 6

TRANSLATIONS OF THE BIBLE

In preaching and writing on Biblical subjects I have generally used the translation of the Bible known as the "King James Version." This is the version that is owned by most people in English-speaking countries. In many ways it has served a grand purpose since it was issued in 1611 A.D. In the study of Biblical doctrine, however, it is sometimes helpful to read and compare some of the other translations that are available to us today.

I sincerely regret that some will be offended because we will refer to other translations beside the King James Version. As one lady said quite dogmatically, *"God* gave the Bible to King James, all other Bibles are of the *Devil!"* Some would agree with the sentiments of Harry Truman (though probably not the *language*) when he said: ". . . I always read the King James Version, not one of those damn new translations that they've got out lately" (p. 231, *Plain Speaking, an Oral Biography of Harry S. Truman*).

I have had people tell me that reading a newer translation, instead of the King James Version, was trying to find the easy way out and that we should be like the reformers—that they never heard of modern-day translations. Very well. But we should also remember that *they never heard of the King James Version either!* Take John Huss, for example. He died in the year 1415 A.D. The King James Version was not printed until the year 1611. William Tyndale died in 1536, Martin Luther in 1546, John Calvin in 1564, John Knox in 1572. All of these noted reformers lived and died before there was any King James Version of the Bible!

Some suppose the King James Version was the *first* English translation of the Bible. But a good while before the King James Version was issued, Wyclif put the Bible into English in around 1384 A.D. (a translation from Latin). The first English translation from the Greek was that made by Tyndale, the title page of which is included in the accompanying illustration.

Several other versions appeared such as the Cloverdale

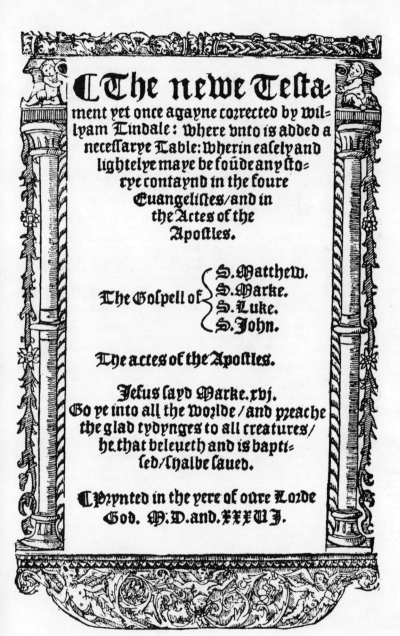

¶The newe Testament yet once agayne corrected by wyllyam Tindale: where vnto is added a necessarye Table: wherin easely and lightelye maye be soūde any storye contaynd in the foure Euangelistes/and in the Actes of the Apostles.

The Gospell of
{
S.Matthew.
S.Marke.
S.Luke.
S.John.
}

The actes of the Apostles.

Jesus sayd Marke.rvj.
Go ye into all the worlde / and preache the glad tydynges to all creatures / he.that beleueth and is baptised/shalbe saued.

¶Prynted in the yere of oure Lorde God. M.D.and.XXVI.

TITLE TO TYNDALE'S TESTAMENT, 1536.

69

The gospell of S. Marke.

The first Chapter.

A

Ｔhis is the begynnynge of the gospell of Jesus Christ the sonne of God, as it is wrytte in the prophetes. Beholde, J sende my messaüger before thy face, which shal prepare thy waye before the. The voyce of a cryer is in the wyldernes: prepare the waye of the LORDE, make his pathes straight.

Jhon was in the wyldernes, and baptysed, and preached the baptyme of amendment, for the remyssion of synnes. And there wente out vnto him the whole londe of Jewry; and they of Jerusalem, and were all baptysed of him in Jordan, and knowleged their synnes.

Jhon was clothed with Camels heer, and with a lethron gerdell aboute his loynes, and ate locustes and wylde hony, and preached, and sayde: There commeth one after me, which is stronger then J: before whom J am not worthy to stoupe downe, and to lowse vp þ lachet of his shue. J baptyse you with water, but he shal baptyse you with the holy goost.

And it happened at the same tyme, that Jesus came out of Galile from Nazareth, and was baptysed of Jhon in Jordan. And as soone as he was come out of the water, he sawe that the heauens opened, and the goost as a doue commynge downe vpon him. And there came a voyce from heaue: Thou art my deare sonne, *in whom J delyte.

And immediatly the sprete droue him in to the wyldernes: and he was in the wyldernes fourtye dayes, and was tempted of Sa

Mal.3.a
zat.11.b
Luc.7.c

Esa.40.a
Mat.3.a
Luc.3.a
Joha.1.b

Joha.3.d

Mat.3.a

Mat.3.b
Luc.3.c
Joha.1.c

Mat.3.b
Luc.3.c
Joha.1.d

Some
reade:
*Jn whõ
J am pa
cified.

Mat.4.a
Luc.4.a

than, and was with the wylde beestes. And the angels mynistred vnto him.

But after that Jhon was taken, Jesus came in to Galile, and preached the gospell of the kyngdome of God, and sayde: the tyme is fulfylled, and the kyngdome of God is at hande: Amende youre selues, and beleue the gospell.

So as he walked by the see of Galile, he sawe Symon and Andrew his brother, castinge their nettes in the see, for they were fysshers. And Jesus sayde vnto the: Folowe me, and J wil make you fysshers of me. And immediatly they left their nettes, and folowed him.

And when he was gone a lytle further from thence, he sawe James the sonne of Zebede, and Jhon his brother, as they were in the shyppe mendynge their nettes. And anone he called them. And they left their father Zebede in the shyppe with the hyred seruauntes, and folowed him.

And they wente in to Capernaum, and immediatly the Sabbathes, he entred in to the synagoge, and taught. And they were astonnyed at his doctryne: for he taught them as one hauynge power, and not as the Scrybes.

And in their synagoge there was a man possessed with a foule sprete, which cried and sayde: Oh what haue we to do with the, thou Jesus of Nazareth. Art thou come to destroye us? J knowe that thou art euen þ holy one of God. And Jesus reproued him, and sayde: holde thy tonge, and departe out of him. And the foule sprete tare him, and cried with a loude voyce, and departed out of him. And they were all astonnyed, in so moch that they axed one another amonge the selues, z sayde: What is this? What new lernynge is this? For he comaundeth the foule spretes with power, and they are obedient vnto him. And immediatly the fame of him was noysed rounde aboute in the coastes and borders of Galile.

And forth with they wente out of the synagoge, and came in to the house of Symõ and Andrew, vh James and Jhon. And Symons mother in lawe laye, z had the feuers, and anone they tolde him of her. And he came to her, and set her vp, and toke her by þ hande, and the feuer left her immediatly, And she mynistred vnto them.

At euen whan the Sonne was gone downe, they brought vnto him all that were sick and possessed, and the whole cite was gathered together at the dore, and

Mat.4.b
Luc.4.b.

Mat.4.c
Luc.5.a

Iere.16.c
Eze.47.b

Luc.4.d
Joha.2.b

Mat.7.c.

C
Luc.4.d

Mat.8.b
Luc.4.d

Mat.8.b
Luc.4.e

CC iiij

(see illustration page 70), the Great Bible, the Geneva Bible, the Bishop's Bible—all of these *before* the King James Version.

Why, then, don't we use one of these translations? There are good reasons why we don't! The English then, as the illustrations show, was quite *different* from the English in use today. Notice the following quotation from Wyclif's translation of Matthew 7:1, 2: "Nyl yee deme, that yee be no demede, for in what dome yee demen, yee schulen be demede." English such as this can hardly be understood today!

Tyndale's translation—over a century later—was more like our English, but still quite different as can be seen by the following quotation from First Corinthians 13: "Though I spake with the tongues of men and angels, and yet had no love, I were even as sounding brasse: or as a tynklynge Cymball. And though I could prophesy, and understoode all secrets . . . yf I had all fayth so that I coulde move mountayns . . . Love suffereth longe, and is corteous . . . reioyseth not in iniquite . . ."

KING JAMES VERSION—1611

Many suppose the text of the King James Version in use today is exactly like that which was issued in 1611. This is *not* so. There were several revisions which followed the original copies issued in 1611—a major revision appeared in 1629, and another edition in 1638. In 1762, an edition was prepared by Thomas Paris of Trinity College, Cambridge, which corrected printing and spelling errors of the former editions and was called the "Standard Edition" of the King James Version. Then in 1769, Benjamin Blayney, a professor of Hebrew at the University of Oxford, revised the spelling, bringing it more up-to-date. This edition was called the Oxford Standard edition. It is the text of *this* edition of the King James Version that is now in common use. Like it or not, even the King James Version is a *revised* version of earlier editions.

Some of the words that appeared in the edition of 1611 which were changed to be understandable are these: fornace was changed to furnace, charet to chariot, murther to murder, damosel to damsel, fet to fetch, creeple to cripple, moneth to month, Moyses to Moses, etc.

For many centuries the English language did not have the word *its*. Though it came into use as early as 1600, many writers resisted "its" as an innovation. It was only gradually eased into the English language. In the original King James Version, Leviticus 25:5 read this way: "That which groweth of *it* own accord of thy harvest thou shalt not reap..." Later printings changed the it to "its." Though "its" appears in only this one verse, it's in there now!

We have included here a reproduction of the title page (see illustration page 73) and a portion of Luke 10 and 11 (see illustration page 74) from the *original* King James Version of 1611. The careful reader will notice the different spelling and type style from our present editions.

Even with the changes that have been made, our present King James Version *still* contains many words which are somewhat obsolete because no longer in common use—words like wot, sith, asswaged, and besom! The following list provides examples of some of these words with the way we would express them today in brackets:

"We *wot* [know] not what is become of him" (Acts 7:40).

"I *trow* [think] not" (Lk. 17:9).

"...*sith* [since] thou hast not hated..." (Ezekiel 35:6).

"He...*scrabbled* [scratched] on the doors of the gate" (1 Sam. 21:13).

"The people *chode* [quarreled, argued] with Moses" (Num. 20:3).

"...and the waters *asswaged* [lessoned, went down]" (Gen. 8:1).

"...old shoes and *clouted* [patched] upon their feet" (Josh. 9:5).

"I will sweep it with the *besom* [broom] of destruction" (Isaiah 14:23).

"Three days *agone* [ago] I fell sick" (1 Sm. 30:13).

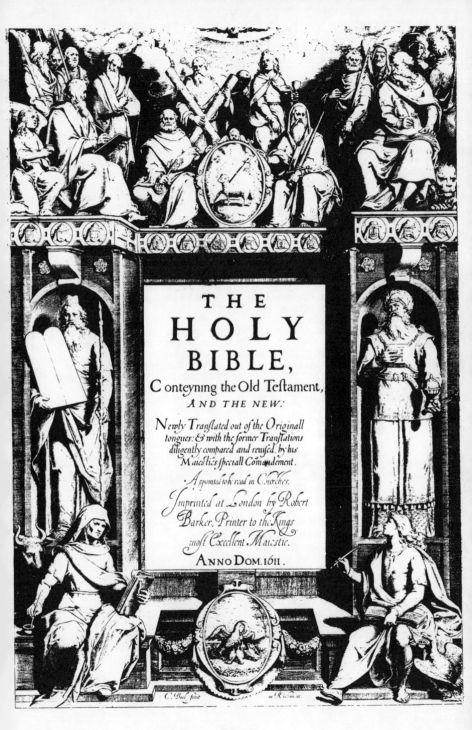

THE
HOLY
BIBLE,

Conteyning the Old Testament,
AND THE NEW:

Newly Translated out of the Originall
tongues: & with the former Translations
diligently compared and reuised, by his
Maiesties speciall Comandement.

Appointed to be read in Churches.

Imprinted at London by Robert
Barker, Printer to the Kings
most Excellent Maiestie.

ANNO DOM. 1611.

C. Boel fecit   in Richmont.

28 And he ſaid vnto him, Thou haſt anſwered right: this do, and thou ſhalt liue.

29 But he willing to iuſtifie himſelfe, ſaid vnto Ieſus, And who is my neighbour?

30 And Ieſus anſwering, ſaid, A certaine man went downe from Hieruſalem to Iericho, and fel among theeues, which ſtripped him of his raiment, and wounded him, and departed, leauing him halfe dead.

31 And by chaunce there came downe a certaine Prieſt that way, and when he ſaw him, he paſſed by on the other ſide.

32 And likewiſe a Leuite, when hee was at the place, came and looked on him, and paſſed by on the other ſide.

33 But a certaine Samaritane as he iourneyed, came where he was; and when hee ſaw him, hee had compaſſion on him,

34 And went to him, and bound vp his wounds, powring in oile and wine, and ſet him on his owne beaſt, and brought him to an Inne, and tooke care of him.

35 And on the morrow when he departed, hee tooke out two ‖ pence, and gaue them to the hoſte, and ſaide vnto him, Take care of him, and whatſoeuer thou ſpendeſt more, when I come againe I will repay thee.

36 Which now of these three, thinkeſt thou, was neighbour vnto him that fell among the theeues?

37 And he ſaid, He that ſhewed mercie on him. Then ſaid Ieſus vnto him, Goe, and doe thou likewiſe.

38 ¶ Now it came to paſſe, as they went, that he entred into a certaine village: and a certaine woman named Martha, receiued him into her houſe.

39 And ſhee had a ſiſter called Mary, which alſo ſate at Ieſus feet, and heard his word.

40 But Martha was cumbred about much ſeruing, and came to him, and ſaid, Lord, doeſt thou not care that my ſiſter hath left mee to ſerue alone? Bid her therefore that ſhe helpe me.

41 And Ieſus anſwered, and ſaide vnto her, Martha, Martha, thou art carefull, and troubled about many things:

42 But one thing is needefull, and Mary hath choſen that good part, which ſhall not bee taken away from her.

‖ See Matt. 20.2.

CHAP. XI.

1 Chriſt teacheth to pray, and that inſtantly: 11 aſſuring that God ſo will giue vs good things. 14 He caſting out a dumbe deuil, rebuketh the blaſphemous Phariſees: 28 and ſheweth who are bleſſed: 29 preacheth to the people, 37 and reprehendeth the outward ſhew of holineſſe in the Phariſees, Scribes and Lawyers.

And it came to paſſe, that as he was praying in a certaine place, when hee ceaſed, one of his diſciples ſaid vnto him, Lord, teach vs to pray, as Iohn alſo taught his diſciples.

2 And hee ſaid vnto them, when ye pray, ſay, * Our Father which art in heauen, Halowed be thy Name, Thy kingdome come, Thy will be done as in heauen, ſo in earth.

* Matth. 6. 9.

3 Giue vs ‖ day by day our dayly bread.

‖ Or, for the day.

4 And forgiue vs our ſinnes: for we alſo forgiue euery one that is indebted to vs. And lead vs not into temptation, but deliuer vs from euill.

5 And he ſaid vnto them, Which of you ſhall haue a friend, and ſhall goe vnto him at midnight, and ſay vnto him, Friend, lend me three loaues.

6 For a friend of mine ‖ in his iourney is come to me, and I haue nothing to ſet before him,

‖ Or, out of his way.

7 And he from within ſhal anſwere and ſay, Trouble mee not, the doore is now ſhut, and my children are with me in bed: I cannot riſe and giue thee.

8 I ſay vnto you, Though he will not riſe, and giue him, becauſe he is his friend: yet becauſe of his importunitie, hee will riſe and giue him as many as he needeth.

9 *And I ſay vnto you, Aſke, and it ſhalbe giuen you: ſeeke, and ye ſhal find: knocke, and it ſhalbe opened vnto you.

* Matth. 7. 7.

10 For euery one that aſketh, receiueth: and he that ſeeketh, findeth: and to him that knocketh, it ſhalbe opened.

11 *If a ſonne ſhall aſke bread of any of you that is a father, will hee giue him a ſtone? Or if he aſke a fiſh, will he for a fiſh giue him a ſerpent?

* Matth. 7. 9.

12 Or if he ſhall aſke an egge, will he offer him a ſcorpion?

13 If ye then, being euill, know how to giue good gifts vnto your children: how much more ſhall your heauenly

Father

"Yet if they shall *bethink* [think, consider] . . . and repent . . ."
(1 Kings 8:47).

"He hath *holpen* [helped] his servant Israel" (Luke 1:54).

"The *haft* [handle] also went in after the blade" (Judges 3:22).

". . . lest he *hale* [haul] thee to the judge, and . . . into prison"
(Lk. 12:58).

"I will *advertise* [tell] thee what this people shall do"
(Num. 24:14).

"They . . . which dwell in the *champaign* [plain]" (Deut. 11:30).

"The oxen . . . that *ear* [plow] the ground . . ." (Is. 30:24).

"Be not carried about with *divers* [different] . . . doctrines"
(Heb. 13:9).

"As *touching* [concerning] the Gentiles which believe . . ."
(Acts 21:25).

"Behold, the noise of the *bruit* [report] is come . . ." (Jer. 10:22).

"The *branch* [song] of the terrible ones shall be brought low"
(Is. 25:5).

"Thy speech *bewrayeth* thee [gives you away]" (Mt. 26:73).

". . . many were *astonied* [dazed, dismayed] at thee"
(Is. 52:14).

A BIBLICAL ACROSTIC

An acrostic is a composition formed by using letters of the
alphabet. If the reader is not familiar with the format of Psalm
119, by turning to this portion he will easily notice it is divided
into 22 sections of eight verses each. The first section is titled
"aleph", the first letter of the Hebrew alphabet. The second section is "beth", the second letter, and on through the letters of the
Hebrew alphabet: aleph, beth, gimel, daleth, he, vau, zain, cheth,
teth, jod, caph, lamed, mem, nun, samech, ain, pe, tzaddi, koph,

resh, schin, and tau. In Hebrew, each of the eight verses within each section begins with the corresponding letter; that is, the first eight verses begin with aleph, the second eight verses with beth, etc.

The following acrostic (though less precise than Psalm 119!) is made up with letters of the alphabet showing some of the words which have a different meaning today than when they were used in the King James Version:

A is for assaying. "The people of God...passed through the Red Sea...which the Egyptians *assaying* to do were drowned" (Heb. 11:29). The word assaying now is commonly used in connection with examination and analysis, as of ore, to determine weight or ingredients. Here it has the meaning of *attempted*. The Egyptians attempted or tried to cross the Red Sea.

B is for becometh. "...receive her in the Lord, as *becometh* saints..." (Rom. 16:1). We might think today of the word "becometh" as expressing a process—as though these people were just in the process of turning into saints. But they were *already* saints (verse 15). That which "becometh" saints would be that which was *becoming*, that which was proper and good. To receive this one in the Lord would be proper and good for saints.

C is for comprehend. "And the light shineth in darkness; and the darkness comprehended it not" (John 1:5). Today we think of the word comprehend as meaning something we can understand. But the meaning here is different, as the Goodspeed translation says concerning the light of God: the darkness "has never *put it out.*"

D is for darling. We commonly use the word "darling" as a term of affection. But in Psalms 35:17, "Rescue...my *darling* from the lions" simply means *life*: save my life.

E is for earnest. We think of a person as being earnest, sincere, serious. It is not so common now to use this word in the sense of a pledge or guarantee, but this was its meaning in Ephesians 1:14: "...the *earnest* of our inheritance." The Holy Spirit is the *guarantee* of our inheritance.

F is for furniture. We think of the term normally in the sense of household furniture. But in Genesis 31:34, it was used of a camel's furniture. "Now Rachel had taken the images, and put them in the camel's *furniture*, and sat upon them." Today we would use the word *saddle*.

G is for governor. "Ships are turned . . . whithersoever the *governor* listeth" (James 3:4). Today we commonly think of the word governor in a political sense. Here James referred to one who steers a ship.

H is for hap. "And [Ruth's] *hap* was to light on a . . . field belonging unto Boaz" (Ruth 2:3). Today, instead of hap, we would say that it *happened* or it was her fortune to come upon this field.

I is for imagination. "They harkened not . . . but walked in the *imagination* of their evil heart" (Jer. 7:24). The meaning here is not the same as we think of the word imagination today. In this reference it means *stubbornness*.

J is for jangling. "Vain *jangling*" (1 Tim. 1:6). We might today associate this word with noise, the sound of a telephone ringing or the like. Here it means vain *discussion*.

K is for knops. "And under the brim of it round about there were knops" (1 Kings 7:24). A more understandable translation for us would be to use the word *gourds*.

L is for leasing. "How long will ye love vanity, and seek after *leasing*?" (Psalms 4:2). Today we think of this word in the sense of leasing or renting a house. The word here means *lies*.

M is for mused. "Men *mused* in their hearts of John, whether he were the Christ" (Lk. 3:15). Today we would say they *wondered*.

N is for neesing. This word is used in Job 41:18. Today, instead of neesing, we would use the word *sneezing*.

O is for ouch. "Thou shalt make *ouches* of gold" (Ek. 28:11, 13). The meaning here is of a *setting* as for a precious stone. We do not normally use the word "ouch" this way today.

P is for purloining. "Exhort servants to be obedient . . . not *purloining*" (Titus 2:9, 10). The meaning is that they were not to *steal*.

Q is for quit. "Then shall he that smote him be *quit*" (Ex. 21:19). This verse explains under which circumstances a man who committed a crime could be quit, or as we would say, *acquitted*.

R is for rereward. "The God of Israel will be your *rereward*" (Isaiah 52:12). This might make us think of the word reward. Like a preacher who didn't know any better said: "The good Lord rewarded me and then he *rerewarded* me!", supposing this was the meaning of rereward. The word here has the meaning of *protection*.

S is for suffer. "Suffer the little children to come unto me" (Mk. 10:14). Today we associate the word suffer with pain. Instead of "suffer", we would simply use the word *let*—"Let the children come."

T is for tire. "Bind the tire of thine head upon thee, and put on thy shoes" (Ezekiel 24:17, 23). Needless to say, this does not refer to an automobile tire! The more recent translations use the word *turban*.

U is for unspeakable. "Thanks be unto God for his *unspeakable* gift" (2 Cor. 9:15). Some today think of the word unspeakable as meaning not permissible. The meaning here is *inexpressible*.

V is for virtue. "...*virtue* had gone out of him" (Mk. 5:30). Today we use the word virtue as meaning moral worth. The meaning here is that *power* went out of Jesus—healing power that was activated by faith.

W is for wit. "We do you to *wit* of the grace of God" (2 Cor. 8:1). We think today of the word wit in connection with humor. But the meaning here is to know or *learn*.

Y is for yesternight. "God...spoke unto me yesternight" (Gen. 31:29). We still commonly use the expression "yesterday", but not yesternight. Today we would simply say *last night*.

A beautiful description of springtime is given in the Song of Solomon, but the mention of the "turtle" has puzzled some. "The winter is past, the rain is over and gone; the flowers appear on the earth; the time of the singing of birds is come, and the voice of the

turtle is heard in our land" (Song of Solomon 2:11, 12). Today we think of a turtle as a slow-moving, voiceless, shelled reptile. But at the time the King James Version was issued, the word "turtle" meant a *bird* and is the same word that is commonly translated "turtle dove." The illustration shows male and female turtledoves.

In the Psalms we read: "The Lord is my shepherd; I shall not *want*", and "They that seek the Lord shall not *want* any good thing" (Ps. 23:1; 34:10). The way "want" is commonly used today, it would sound like those who seek the Lord don't want any *good* thing. What do they want? Bad things? No, of course not. "Lack" is the word we would use now. Those who follow the Lord will not *lack*.

At the marriage at Cana, to which Jesus and his disciples were invited, we are told that "they *wanted* wine" (John 2:3). The meaning is, as the context shows, they ran out of wine, they *lacked* wine. With the turning of water into wine by Jesus, they were able to continue serving wine to the guests.

How much wine was produced on this occasion? There were six pots which contained two or three *firkins* each. A "firkin" is about nine gallons, making the total amount somewhere between 108 and 142 gallons of wine. If we figure 10 ounces as an average size serving, this would be 1,382 to 1,818 glasses of wine served after the other wine ran out. It has been said that either each person drank a lot of wine, there were many guests at the wedding, or (as when Jesus multiplied the loaves) there was a supply left over.

In Esther 3:13 we read: "And the letters were sent by *posts* into all the king's provinces." Today we would probably speak of "postmen", as the word "post" would cause most to think of a fence post. Still, we can't fail to notice the similarity of wording in words such as postal service or post office. On the other hand, the word "mail" (which we would normally associate with the post office) when used in the King James Version refers to *armor* (1 Sam. 17:5, 38).

When we read that the Psalmist "*prevented* the dawning of the morning" (Psalms 119:147), it sounds as though he hindered or stopped the sun from coming up! The actual meaning is simply that he arose early.

"He who now letteth will *let*" (2 Thess. 2:7). At the time the King James Version was translated, the word "let" meant "to hinder." As Paul told the Romans, he had intended to come to them "but was *let* hitherto" (Rom. 1:13)—he was hindered in coming to them. Today, the word "let" is used in almost an *opposite* sense. If we let someone do something, this means we allow it—not hinder it!

Since language is a moving thing, since words can go through changes of meaning over a period of time, a good *translation* (not just a paraphrase) in modern English can be helpful to the serious Bible student.

ANCIENT OMISSIONS OR ADDITIONS

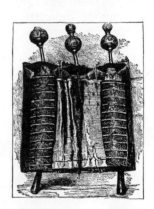

Because words in one language may not have an exact equivalent in another language, translators sometimes face a problem in deciding how to convey the proper meaning. Not only this, but sometimes there are variations in the ancient manuscripts from which they seek to translate. The omission or addition of one word can make a different meaning. The following verses provide two interesting examples of this:

(1) "Thou hast multiplied the nation, and *not* increased the joy; they joy before thee according to the joy in harvest, and as men rejoice when they divide the spoil" (Isaiah 9:3). Notice the word "not." The setting here is one of joy, yet the use of the word "not"

throws the whole idea into conflict. Do the oldest manuscripts we have available today have the word "not" in them? Some do, some do not. Many scholars believe, and I think with good reason, that the word "not" was not in the original text of Isaiah. The meaning, within context, is that God had multiplied the nation *and increased the joy*.

(2) "God judgeth the righteous, and God is angry with the wicked every day" (Psalms 7:11). This is the reading given in the King James Version. But some ancient manuscripts include the word "not"; that is, "God is *not* angry every day." The Syriac: "God is the Judge of righteousness; he is not angry every day." The Vulgate: "God is a Judge, righteous, strong, and patient;—will he be angry every day?" The Septuagint: "God is a righteous Judge, strong and longsuffering; not bringing forth his anger every day." Similar readings are given in the Arabic and Ethiopic manuscripts. In all fairness, it is true there are other manuscripts, also very ancient, which read as the King James Version. But the mass of evidence supports the reading which includes the word "not."

DETAILS CLARIFIED

Translations in modern English have sometimes clarified certain details that a person might overlook in reading the King James Version only. A good example of this may be seen in the healing of the lame man in Acts 3. Have we not usually pictured him as being healed while he sat begging at the gate of the temple? The Bible does say this is where he was placed each day to beg. But when he encountered Peter and John, he was being *carried* along. Let me give this passage from the Phillips' version:

"One afternoon Peter and John were on their way to the Temple for the three o'clock hour of prayer. A man who had been lame from birth was being CARRIED along in the crowd, for it was the daily practice to put him down at what was known as the Beautiful Gate of the temple, so that he could beg from the people as they went in . . ." (Acts 3:1).

All of the translations I have checked show that the lame man was being carried along when he saw Peter and John. If we look again at the King James Version, it can be seen there also, though it is not as noticeable: "And a certain man lame from his mother's womb was *carried*, whom they laid daily at the gate of the temple . . . ''

The reader will recall the account of the shipwreck which occurred while Paul was being taken to Rome. At one point we read: '' . . . when they had taken up the anchors, they committed themselves unto the sea'' (Acts 27:40). This sounds as though they jumped overboard into the sea. But they did not do this until later, as the context unmistakably shows. In view of this, the marginal rendering is preferable which says they ''cut the anchors and they left *them* in the sea''—the anchors. Newer translations all clarify this point, such as Moffatt's version which says the *''anchors* were cut away and left in the sea.''

A well-known verse from the book of Psalms says: ''I will lift up mine eyes unto the hills, from whence cometh my help'' (Psalms 121:1). Some suppose these words refer to the peace and solitude one might experience by time spent in a beautiful setting of hills or mountains. But this is not the point here.

Instead of the hills being the source of help for the Psalmist, the very next verse says: ''My help cometh *from the Lord.''* A few verses later we read: ''Unto *thee* lift I up mine eyes'' (Psalms 123:1). He was looking to the Lord for help—not to the hills. Because of this, some prefer the reading: ''I will lift up mine eyes ABOVE the hills, from whence cometh my help. My help cometh from the Lord.'' Then there is harmony and a good sense. The *New English Bible* says: ''If I lift up my eyes to the hills, where shall I find help? Help comes only from the Lord, maker of heaven and earth.''

Taking the verse within its context, it is clear that the writer was not saying in one verse he was looking to the hills for help and then state in the very next verse that his help was from the Lord!

In Matthew 19:24 we read: ''It is easier for a camel to go through the eye of a needle . . . '' The Lamsa translation says: ''It is easier for a ROPE to go through the eye of a needle.'' In the Greek, ''camel'' and ''cable'' (rope) are almost alike. Consequently, some old manuscripts have cable, though the bulk of evidence is probably in favor of the word camel as in the King James Version.

SPIRIT OR GHOST?

I have known people who believe there is a difference between the holy "Spirit" and the holy "Ghost." A woman who believes this way told a preacher I know: "Well, you *may* have the Holy *Spirit*, but if you get the Holy GHOST it is really good!" Some think such a distinction is indicated in John 7:39: "This spake he [Jesus] of the *Spirit*, which they that believe on him should receive: for the Holy *Ghost* was not yet given..." But the word "Spirit" and the word "Ghost" are *exactly the same word* in the Greek (pneuma). Why the King James translators were not uniform in their translation of this word is difficult to say. In the minds of many, the word "ghost" has come to have a spooky meaning—as though it were the spirit of a dead person. Consequently, the expression "Holy *Spirit*" actually better conveys the meaning that was intended by the writers of the New Testament.

LOST AXE HEAD

The King James Version regarding the lost axe head reads as follows: "As one was felling a beam, the axe head fell into the water; and he cried, and said, Alas, master! for it was borrowed. And the man of God [Elisha] said, Where fell it? And he shewed him the place. And he cut down a stick and cast it in thither; and the iron did swim [surface]. Therefore said he, Take it up to thee. And he put out his hand, and took it" (2 Kings 6:5-7).

According to George M. Lamsa, noted translator of the Bible from Aramaic manuscripts, the iron came to the top of the water because Elisha stuck the stick into the hole of the axe head. The miracle was in the fact that the prophet was guided to the exact spot so that when he stuck the stick into the muddy water it went right into the axe head. So, from the Aramaic text, Lamsa translates this verse as follows: "And he cut off a stick and thrust it in there; and it *stuck in the hole of the axehead.*"

If this is the correct meaning, it would provide a good explanation as to why a stick was used. Had God intended the iron to simply swim to the surface where it could be recovered, why would any stick be required at all? I don't know. I mention this point only as food for thought. It would be useless to make it a dogma.

SAMSON AT LEHI

We are all familiar, of course, with the exploits of Samson, including the time he slew a thousand Philistines with the jawbone of an ass. There is one part of this story, however, that has commonly been overlooked.

We are told that when Samson "came unto Lehi...he found a new jawbone...and slew a thousand men therewith. And Samson said, With the jawbone...have I slain a thousand men. And it came to pass, when he had made an end of speaking, that he cast away the jawbone out of his hand, and called the place Ramath-lehi (casting away of the jawbone). And he was sore athirst, and called on the Lord...God clave an hollow place that was *in the jaw* (lehi), and there came water thereout; and when he had drunk...he revived: wherefore he called the name thereof En-hakkore (the well of him that called), which is in Lehi unto this day" (Judges 15:14-19).

This wording (as given in the King James Version) would lead us to believe that Samson drank the water out of the jaw itself. The margin, however, reads that "God clave an hollow place that was in *Lehi*" as verses 9, 14, 17. Actually, this area came to be called Lehi (Jawbone) because of the incident that happened here with the jawbone. The word translated "jaw" or "jawbone" is *Lehi* all the way through this passage. Consequently, when we come to that portion which says that "God clave an hollow place that was in the jaw", it could just as correctly be translated "Lehi"—the name of the *place*. The word is the same. What, then, are our reasons for believing that the water came from an opening in the ground at this area called Lehi (Jawbone), rather than from the jawbone itself?

There are several reasons. We notice that Samson named this place from which he drank *En-hakkore*, the *well* of him that called. It was actually a well or spring of water that resulted when God clave an hollow place that was in Lehi. To this the writer of Judges adds: "...which is in *Lehi* unto this day." Commenting on this phrase, Adam Clarke says: "...consequently not IN the jaw-bone of the ass, a most unfortunate rendering"(Vol. 2, p. 166).

The Goodspeed version gives a good rendering of this portion

84

in these words: "Then God split open the mortar that is at Lehi, and water gushed out of it; and when he drank, his spirits rose, and he revived. That is how its name came to be called En-hakkor (the spring of the caller), which is at Lehi to this day."

The Barnes commentary (p. 455) makes the following statement: "The right translation is, 'the hollow place which is in *Lehi.*' The word translated 'hollow place', means a mortar (Prov. 27:22), and is here evidently a hollow or basin among the cliffs of Lehi, which, from its shape, was called 'the mortar'...A spring, on the way from Socho to Eleutheropolis, was commonly called Samson's spring in the time of St. Jerome."

The *Pulpit Commentary* states very clearly that it was a spring in the ground which provided the water.

Josephus, writing in the first century, said this: "And when he (Samson) came to a certain place, which is now called the Jaw-bone, on account of the great action there performed by Samson, though of old it had no particular name at all...Samson broke his bonds asunder, and catching up the jaw-bone of an ass...fell upon his enemies, and smiting them with his jaw-bone, slew a thousand of them...God was moved with his entreaties, and raised up a plentiful fountain of sweet water at a certain rock; whence it was that Samson called the place the Jaw-bone (Lehi), and so it is called to this day" (Josephus, Book 5, 8:8, 9).

In view of this evidence, we do not believe that after Samson "cast away the jawbone out of his hand" he went and picked it up again to get a drink out of it. Instead, the correct translation and meaning is that God clave an hollow place in Lehi. It was from this spring or fountain that he drank and which he named En-hakkore (meaning "the well of him that called") and of which it was stated, "it is in Lehi unto this day."

RAVENS OR ARABIANS?

Something else we should notice in our study of translation is that the original Hebrew words were written without vowels. In the case of Elijah, depending on how vowels are supplied, he could have been fed by ravens—or Arabians! But before going into this, we will notice the passage as given in the King James Version:

"And the word of the Lord came unto him [Elijah], saying, Get thee hence, and turn thee eastward, and hide thyself by the brook Cherith, that is before Jordan. And it shall be, that thou shalt drink of the brook; and I have commanded the *ravens* to feed thee there . . . And the *ravens* brought him bread and flesh in the morning, and bread and flesh in the evening; and he drank of the brook" (1 Kings 17:2-6).

The Hebrew word translated "ravens", without vowels, is *rbm*. Depending on how the vowels are added, it could mean ravens, Arabians, merchants, or the people of a town named Orbo! For comparison we can take the word "spoon." Without vowels it is *spn*. By adding vowels to these letters we could form spoon, spin, span, spun, or spine.

Adam Clarke says that if we take *rbm* to mean ravens, "we shall find any interpretation on this ground to be clogged with difficulties." The raven, for one thing, is listed in Leviticus 11:13-15 as an unclean bird: "And these ye shall have in abomination among the fowls . . . every raven." Does it seem most likely that God would use a bird that was considered unclean and an abomination to bring food to his chosen prophet?

Carrion, the putrefying flesh of a carcass, is the food of ravens. It is self-evident that this type of food was not that which would have been brought to the prophet. Of course, a miracle could have changed the nature of the bird so that it would pick up some other food, perhaps from someone's table at a distance. Then, by another miracle, the bird could give up the food to the prophet. If this is indeed what happened, it seems a lot was required to accomplish one simple purpose. What, then, are the alternatives to this viewpoint?

The word translated "ravens" in the King James Version could be translated "merchants." Some believe that certain people who traveled and traded through that part of the land were inspired to provide food for the prophet. We do know that *oreby*, the contracted form of the word translated "ravens" in the King James Version, has the meaning of merchants in Ezekiel 27:9, 27.

Others believe the correct translation would be "Arabians"—that people from Arab colonies in that area fed Elijah. They could have been inhabitants of a town by the name of Orbo—another possible translation. This is the view expressed in the Arabic Version. An old rabbinical commentary on Genesis mentions such a town: "There is a town in the vicinity of Beth-shan, and its name is Orbo." Jerome, who lived in the fourth century, was familiar with this place. He spent several years in Palestine during which he studied the geography, customs, and language of that land. His statement about the people of Orbo is, we feel, especially weighty: "The Orbim, inhabitants of a town in the confines of the Arabs, gave nourishment to Elijah."

Long-held ideas are not quickly discarded, nor do we insist that anyone give up the idea of ravens. It has only been our intention here to point out why ravens may not have been the original meaning in this passage. It is apparent that as far as the original word used, it is capable of different meanings and this example shows one of the problems translators face because originally the manuscripts did not have vowels.

PUNCTUATION

Another problem is that the original manuscripts were written when there were no punctuation marks. Consequently, commas and question marks must be inserted as the translators think best—based on their beliefs. Usually the correct punctuation is indicated by the wording, but there are a few passages in which a change of comma location can change the meaning; the classic example being the dispute over Luke 23:43.

The actual word-for-word translation of this verse in English (without punctuation) is as follows: "Verily I say unto you today thou shalt be with me in paradise." The accompanying illustra-

tion shows this verse in the Greek from which the New Testament was translated. There are no commas or punctuation marks. Letters all run together. Where the comma is placed in translating into English could make it read: "Verily I say unto you today, thou shalt be with me in paradise", or "Verily I say unto you, Today thou shalt be with me in paradise". If a question mark was added, it could read: "Verily I say unto you today, Shalt thou be with me in paradise?"

Does this verse mean the thief would be with Jesus that same day in paradise, or does it mean that on that very day Jesus was assuring him that he would be with him in paradise—regardless of where or when? Since the position of the comma would make this difference, and since there were no commas in the original, doctrines on the state of the dead cannot honestly be built on this one verse—one way or the other.

COMMAND GOD?

One more example involving punctuation will be given; this one concerning a question mark. In Isaiah 45:11 we read: "Concerning the work of my hands *command ye me.*" Does this mean we are to command God what to do? People have commanded God to heal them, have commanded God to meet their need, have commanded God to do this or that. We realize that in prayer we "ask" God; but somehow the idea that we are to "command" God seems out of place.

We believe this statement was intended as a *question.* Notice Moffatt's translation: "Would you dictate to me about my work?" Or Goodspeed: "Will you question me concerning my children or give me orders regarding the work of my hands?" We believe a question mark is correct (as in these translations) because this is the indication of the context.

We are told that the Lord is God and there is none else; he has created all things: light, darkness, good, evil (verses 6, 7). "Woe unto him that striveth with his Maker!...Shall the clay say to him that fashioneth it, What makest thou?" (verse 9). "Woe unto him that saith unto his father, What begettest thou? or to the woman, What hast thou brought forth?" (verse 10). The greatness of God is further seen in verse 12 in that he is the creator of earth, of heaven, and of man. The point, then, in verse 11 is: Who is man to try to command God or dictate to him what he must do?

The meaning is not that we should "command God" (as some have preached), for as the context points out, he is the potter and we are the clay. Since the clay does not command the potter concerning the work of his hands, so Isaiah 45:11 is best understood as a question—not as an admonition to order God what to do!

88

Chapter 7

DIVINE HEALING—
WHAT DOES THE BIBLE REALLY SAY?

As we approach the subject of healing, it should be stated at the outset that we have no doubts about the power and ability of God to heal. Anyone who could create this great world and make man in his own image is certainly able to heal. We believe God heals and rejoice with those who are healed through faith. I have never believed that healing passed away with the death of the apostles, as though God's healing power was exhausted on some former generation. But there are some things regarding healing which have been commonly misunderstood.

Some believe it is always God's will to heal all people at all times. They point out that multitudes came to Jesus and he healed "all" that were sick (Mt. 8:16). Since Jesus Christ is the same yesterday, today, and forever (Heb. 13:8), it is still his will and purpose to heal all that are sick. Not only this, he actually took stripes upon his back to pay for man's healing (2 Peter 2:24). Thus, it is believed, healing from sickness is just as much in the atonement as salvation from sin. And not only is it always God's will to heal the sick—if a person will serve God he will never even get sick; he will have divine health.

Now all of this *sounds good*, but is it *good sound doctrine*? To get right to the very heart of the matter, we should consider first of all the Biblical teaching regarding the atonement.

IS HEALING IN THE ATONEMENT?

The Biblical verses which are quoted to support the doctrine of healing in the atonement are as follows:

"Himself took our infirmities, and bare our sicknesses" (Matt. 8:17) and "By whose stripes ye were healed" (1 Peter 2:24)— both verses being quotations from the book of Isaiah (53:4, 5).

If we will examine these verses within the New Testament *context* in which they were quoted, however, it will be seen that neither verse supports the idea that healing from physical sickness is in the atonement of Christ. First, notice the passage in

Matthew:

"When the even was come, they brought unto him [Jesus] many that were possessed with devils: and he cast out the spirits with his word, and healed all that were sick: that it might be fulfilled which was spoken by Esaias the prophet, saying, Himself took our infirmities, and bare our sicknesses."

The reference here is unmistakably to the healing of actual, physical sicknesses by Jesus. But did Matthew apply this verse to the atonement? No, he did not. According to Matthew, Jesus fulfilled these words by his healing ministry. *When* was this verse fulfilled? "When the even was come..." *Where* was it fulfilled? At *Capernaum* (verse 5)—not Calvary or Jerusalem. If our Lord's healing ministry fulfilled the words of Isaiah—as when he healed at Capernaum—it is clear that Matthew did not regard these words as a reference to the atonement.

The other verse which is quoted to support the doctrine of healing in the atonement is 1 Peter 2:24: "By whose stripes ye were healed." In this case, the redemptive work of Christ is definitely in view, mention being made of his sufferings, of bearing our sins in his body on the tree, and his death at Calvary. But *what kind* of healing was provided by these stripes? In this case, the healing mentioned was not physical healing, but spiritual. The reader will quickly notice from the context that Peter applied this verse to *healing from sin*, not physical sickness.

"Who his own self bare our sins in his own body on the tree, that we, being dead to sins, should live unto righteousness: by whose stripes ye were healed. FOR—notice it!—FOR ye were as sheep going astray; but are now returned unto the Shepherd and Bishop of your souls" (1 Peter 2:24, 25). The word "for"—a connective word—clearly shows that Peter understood this as spiritual healing. Those who, as sheep, had gone astray were healed by his stripes and thus returned to God. They were healed *spiritually*. The application is clear and simple.

This does not mean, of course, that Peter did not believe in healing for the sick—physically. Many people were healed through his ministry, including the lame man who begged at the Gate Beautiful. Others were healed as his shadow passed over them. The dead were raised also. Peter believed in healing and miracles.

Yet, when he quoted the verse about the healing stripes, he did not apply it to physical healing, but to spiritual healing from sin.

Peter was not out of line in applying Isaiah's words this way. It was in a *spiritual* sense that Isaiah repeatedly spoke of healing. The words "heal", "healed", "healer", "healing", "healeth", and "health" appear in Isaiah a total of nine times. None refer specifically to bodily healing.

SPIRITUAL HEALING

In Isaiah 3:7, a "healer" was one who would become a ruler to heal Jerusalem and Judah from national calamity. In Isaiah 6:10, Isaiah was told to speak and warn the people that their cities were marked for destruction, yet in this spiritually sick condition they would not "convert, and be healed." In Isaiah 9:22, Egyptians would come to know the Lord, "and they shall return even to the Lord, and he shall be intreated of them, and shall heal them." Spiritual healing—returning to the Lord—is clearly intended. Isaiah 30:26 speaks of a national healing, not physical healing of individuals: "In the day that the Lord bindeth up the breach of his people, and healeth the stroke of their wound . . ." Isaiah 57: 17, 18: "I have seen his ways, and will heal him . . . Peace, peace to him that is afar off . . . I will heal him." This is spiritual healing. Isaiah 58:8 says that if the house of Jacob would turn from evil, "then shall thy light break forth as the morning and thine health shall spring forth speedily: and thy righteousness shall go before thee"—another reference to spiritual healing. And, according to Peter, it was spiritual healing that was intended by the words of Isaiah 53:5, "With his stripes we are healed."

Often—though of course not always—Old Testament healing promises were for *spiritual* healing. "Bless the Lord, O my SOUL, and forget not all his benefits: who forgiveth all thine iniquities; who healeth all *thy* diseases" (Psalms 103:2, 3). This verse is commonly used in connection with physical healing. But that David was speaking of the *soul* being healed is apparent. It was healing in a spiritual sense. Psalms 41:4 is a parallel passage: "Heal my SOUL; *for* I have *sinned* against thee."

I do not point these things out as a denial of healing for the *physical* body. I have personally prayed for several thousand sick

sick people over the years. If God can answer any prayer at all, why not one for a person who is sick? Healing through prayer is very clearly taught in James 5:15 and other verses.

Why, then, do we challenge the belief that healing from sickness is just as much in the atonement as salvation from sin? This is why: there have been many very fine Christians who were physically afflicted. Some have had the confession until the day they died that they were just as much healed as they were saved—since both were in the atonement. Yet they died with afflictions; they were not healed. I cannot be honest and ignore this. I have seen too many cases. My concern in pointing this out is, I feel, a valid concern. People who are taught in a dogmatic way that bodily healing is *just as much* in the atonement as salvation commonly face a problem when they are not healed. They reason: If healing from sickness is just as much in the atonement as salvation from sin, why am I not healed? Maybe I am not saved either! If I am not fully healed, perhaps I am not fully forgiven! In some cases worry and mental conflict about *why* a person is not healed can become worse than the physical affliction.

In one sense we believe that *all* good things are found in Christ and his redemptive work. But the teaching that healing from bodily sickness is *just as much* in the atonement as salvation from sin is simply not true.

NOT ONE FEEBLE PERSON

Some believe that when the Israelites partook of the passover they were all healed, for we are told that after coming out of Egypt, "there was not one feeble person among their tribes." And since that passover was a type of Christ and his redemptive work, physical healing must be included in the atonement. But were all the Israelites healed when they came out of Egypt?

It is true that Psalms 105:37 tells us that God brought forth the Israelites from Egypt, "and there was not ONE FEEBLE PERSON among their tribes." Many books on divine healing use this scripture as a proof text that all of the Israelites were healed when they came out of Egypt. But this verse has nothing to do

92

with healing! The *real* reason why there were no feeble people among their tribes was because all that were feeble were KILLED in battle!

Turning to the Biblical record, we read exactly what happened to those that were feeble. "Remember what Amalek did unto thee by the way, when ye were come forth out of Egypt; how he met thee by the way, and smote the hindmost of thee, even ALL THAT WERE FEEBLE behind thee, when thou wast faint and weary; and he feared not God" (Deut. 25:17, 18).

If we read just Psalms 105:37 alone—about no feeble people among their tribes—one guess might be as good as another as to *why* there were no feeble people. But what happened to them is clearly stated. In battle with Amalek, when the people were faint and weary, those that were feeble were killed. They had not all be healed.

93

That there were those who experienced healing in the wilderness journey (Numbers 21:9; 12:13) and that they were given healing promises (Exodus 15:26; 23:25) is apparent. But that there were those among the Israelites which were afflicted with blindness, deafness, lameness, and other diseases is definitely implied from Leviticus 19:14, 21:18-20. Those with diseases such as leprosy, whether male or female, were put outside the camp (Numbers 5:2-4). All were not healed.

JESUS CHRIST THE SAME...

The Bible says: "Jesus Christ the same yesterday, and today, and for ever" (Heb. 13:8). There is a grand truth here—the truth of an unchanging Christ in a changing world! But does this mean, as we have sometimes taken it to mean, that Jesus always heals to the same extent and in the same ways at all times? The answer to this is *clear* in the scriptures.

Two thousand years ago Jesus healed multitudes of people, including many lepers (Lk. 7:22). He was the "same" in the days of Elisha, but *how many* lepers were healed then? According to the words of Jesus himself, only *one* leper was healed. "Many lepers were in Israel in the time of Eliseus [Elisha] the prophet; and none of them was cleansed, saving Naaman" (Lk. 4:27).

It was not that God was unmindful of lepers, for during that same period four lepers marched into the Syrian camp only to find it forsaken, "for the Lord had made the host of the Syrians to hear a noise of chariots, and a noise of horses, even the noise of a great host" (2 Kings 7:6). These lepers were blessed—with silver, gold, and clothes in abundance—but they were not healed. Jesus Christ was the "same" in those days, yet only Naaman was healed. Think it through.

Jesus healed many blind people in his earthly ministry, even a man *born* blind. Jesus had been the "same" all through human history, but had anyone ever been healed that was born blind before? The words of the blind man that was healed imply that his healing was a "first" and the Pharisees, who were reasonably acquainted with Old Testament history, offered no rebuttal. "Since the world began was it not heard that any man opened the eyes of one that was born blind" (John 9:32). Christ was the "same" since the world began, but we do not read of any who

94

were born blind that were healed through the 4,000 years of Old Testament history.

Of all the 39 books of the Old Testament, only a few mention anyone being healed. But in his earthly ministry, Jesus healed multitudes. There was a continuing move of the Spirit within the early church. The Lord who is the same yesterday, today, and forever, worked with them and confirmed the word with signs following. And the history of the church since that time has recorded outstanding instances of healing through faith. However, it is also true that there have been periods when there have been more spiritual results than others, times of greater visitation, times of refreshing from the presence of the Lord. Does this mean, then, that Jesus Christ changes? No, he is the same. But this does not, and cannot, mean that he always heals in the same way or to the same extent at all times. Hebrews 13:8 contains a powerful truth, but unless we keep it in a proper scriptural *balance*, we are forced to an extreme which neither fits the overall testimony of scripture or the actual experience of believers.

HEALING ABOVE ALL THINGS?

I have heard Third John 2 used in the following manner: "God says to us, 'Beloved, I wish above all things that thou mayest prosper *and* be in health, *even as thy soul* prospereth.' God wants us to be in health *physically* as much as he wants our soul to prosper *spiritually*." This was never the intended meaning of this verse.

First of all, this was not a message from *God* to the individual believer. It was simply a form of greeting from a pastor to his close friend Gaius, as we see in verse one. Considered as a *greeting*, it is clear that it cannot rightly be used as a basis for *dogma*. Nor does it teach that physical health and prosperity are as important as the prosperity of the soul. The actual meaning of this verse comes through clearly in the Goodspeed translation which we will give for comparison: "The Elder to my dear friend Gaius, whom I truly love. Dear friend, it is my prayer that everything is going well with you and that you are well; I know it is well with your soul."

Let me hasten to add that Third John 2 is a wonderful verse. I have quoted it often. I would not discourage anyone from deriving inspiration or faith for a financial need, a healing touch, or some other need from God by the use of this verse. But for our present purpose, it has been necessary to show this verse within its actual setting.

Some believe that if people are fully serving God, they will not even get sick! But I have known of men who worked so hard for *God* they suffered a collapse. One example of this is even found in the Bible. Epaphroditus, who worked with Paul in the gospel ministry, "was sick nigh unto death" (Phil. 2:27, 30).

The idea that if one gets sick he has *failed* God has led to all kinds of judging, perplexity, and doubts. But again, if we go to the scriptures, we can see this is an extremist position. We know that Elisha was a man of faith and miracles. Nevertheless, we read that "Elisha was fallen *sick* of his sickness whereof he *died*" (2 Kings 13:14, 20). He was not healed. Had he lost out with God? No, he had not! As we continue reading, God even honored him to the extent that a dead man was raised to life by merely touching his bones. "And it came to pass, as they were burying a man, that, behold, they spied a band of men; and they cast the man into the sepulchre of Elisha: and when the man was let down, and touched the bones of Elisha, he revived, and stood up on his feet"(2 Kings 13:21).

A BIBLICAL BALANCE

Just because we believe in divine healing, we need not accept the extremism with which the doctrine has been plagued. There have been many abuses. There are preachers who become quite arrogant about the idea that it is always God's will to heal. They have not always been totally honest, for in their "faith preaching" they have usually only told the success stories and results have been grossly exaggerated. Some have preached against doctors or any medical help. After all, as they claim, if healing is just as much in the atonement as salvation, who would need medical science for anything! Because of such teachings, there have been some sad cases—some in which people have died needlessly. I could relate a number of these cases that I know of personally.

Unless we choose to blank it out of our minds, we must admit there are many fine, dedicated Christians who suffer with one or more afflictions. Some are healed; some are not. Some may be healed of one thing, yet not another. When people do not receive healing, some would tell them they do not have *faith* or that there is *sin* in their lives. To throw such stones, to make such excuses, is but the result to which an unbalanced view of healing has led. If we are Bible believers, if we believe in Bible preaching, then why not believe in the Biblical balance regarding healing? Since sickness is all a part of the curse, then any way by which it is overcome—through surgery, climate, diet, medicine, exercise, or prayer!—is certainly within the framework of God's abundant provision.

JESUS AND PRAYER FOR THE SICK

At first thought, the following statement may come as a surprise, but it is a fact: *Jesus did not pray for the sick*. We should clarify this. Jesus *healed* the sick, but we have no record of him actually praying for the sick. *Prayer* for the sick is scriptural of course (James 5:15), but the gift of healing in the life of Jesus was *so powerful* that just a word or the touch of his hand brought healing. Some were healed by simply touching him in faith. Such was the case of the woman with an issue of blood.

TOUCHING CHRIST IN FAITH

In keeping with our overall theme in this book, we will notice some of the less-known things regarding the woman who touched the hem of Jesus' garment and was healed. We are told that she "had suffered many things of many physicians, and had *spent all that she had*, and was nothing bettered, but rather grew *worse*" (Mk. 5:26). We quickly read over these words, perhaps without thinking of the primitive state of medical knowledge at that time. With this serious female problem, it is not difficult to understand the embarrassment, frustration, pain, and rejection, as well as the loss of money involved, as she "suffered *many* things of *many* physicians."

"And when the woman saw that she was not hid, she came *trembling*, and falling down before him, she declared unto him before all the people for what cause she had touched him, and how she was healed immediately" (Lk. 8:47). Here, again, there is a point that is sometimes overlooked. Why was she *trembling*? According to the law of Moses, "a woman with an issue of her blood" was ritually unclean and anything she touched was unclean. It is all spelled out in Leviticus 15:25-28. For her, in this condition, to press through and touch the garment of Jesus would have brought severe rebuke by the Jewish legalists. Knowing the strictness of the Jews for certain fine points of the law, we can understand at least one reason why this woman was "trembling."

But Jesus did not rebuke her. Love was stronger than law; her need more important to Jesus than ceremonial ritual. "Daughter", Jesus said, "be of good comfort: thy faith hath made thee whole; go in peace" (Lk. 8:48). Tradition has assigned the name Veronica to this woman, but this is tradition only.

Jesus said to this woman: "*Thy* faith hath made thee whole." Some put the emphasis on the fact it was *her* faith. Consequently, they believe that *only* those who have faith can be healed. While it is good and proper to have faith, this was not always required in the healing ministry of Jesus. What about the dead that were raised? Did they exercise faith at a certain moment? Did those who were insane perform some certain faith ritual to be healed? Or what about Malchus? Peter had cut this man's right ear off. He was among those working against Jesus. He had neither faith for healing nor was he a believer in Jesus Christ. Nevertheless, the healing power of God extended even to him (Lk. 22:51).

AN UNUSUAL HEALING

Finally, we will notice one of the seldom-mentioned healings of Jesus. It is found only in Mark 7:32-35. Unlike the healing in which Jesus *spit* and made clay to anoint the eyes of the blind man (John 9), in this passage—at least at first glance—it would appear that Jesus spit and touched the man's tongue. "And they bring unto him one that was deaf, and had an impediment in his speech...and he took him aside from the multitude, and put his fingers into his ears, and he spit, and touched his tongue; and looking up to heaven, he sighed, and saith unto him, Ephphatha, that is, Be opened. And straightway his ears were opened, and the string of his tongue was loosed, and he spake plain."

One reason this passage is seldom quoted (and, consequently, little-known) is because the method employed seems repulsive by our standards today. But perhaps we have not rightly understood this incident. In closing this chapter, I will simply ask the reader to consider the following view of Adam Clarke, written over 150 years ago, regarding this unusual healing: "It is possible that what is attributed here to *Christ* belongs to the *person* who was cured. I will give my sense of the place in a short paraphrase. *And* Jesus *took him aside from the multitude: and* [the deaf man] *put his fingers into his ears*, intimating thereby to Christ that they were so stopped that he could not hear; *and having spat out*, that there might be nothing remaining in his mouth to offend the sight when Christ should look at his tongue, *he touched his tongue*, showing to Christ that it was so bound that he could not speak: *and he looked up to heaven*, as if to implore assistance from above: *and he groaned*, being distressed because of his present affliction, and thus emplored relief: for, not being able to *speak*, he could only *groan* and *look up*, expressing by these signs, as well as he could, his *afflicted state*, and the *desire* he had to be relieved. *Then* Jesus, having compassion upon him, said, *Be opened*, so that he could hear distinctly; and the *impediment* to his speaking was removed, so that *he spake properly*. The original will admit of this interpretation; and this, I am inclined to believe is the true meaning of this otherwise (to me and many others) unaccountable passage" (*Clark's Commentary, Vol. 5, 313).

*   *   *   *   *

Success comes in "cans": failure in "can'ts." Those who can — do; those who can't — criticize.

*   *   *   *   *

Pick your friends, but not to pieces. You can't spell "brothers" and not spell "others." It is better to say a good thing about a bad fellow than to say a bad thing about a good fellow.

*   *   *   *   *

Worry is like a rocking chair. It will give you something to do, but it won't get you anywhere.

Chapter 8

BIBLICAL AWARENESS

Enclosed in the box below is an awareness test. First read the sentence. Now count the F's in the sentence. Count them only once; do not go back and count them again.

> FINISHED FILES ARE THE RE-
> SULT OF YEARS OF SCIENTIF-
> IC STUDY COMBINED WITH THE
> EXPERIENCE OF MANY YEARS.

There are six F's. However, because the F in "of" sounds like a V, it seems to disappear, and most will count only three F's in the sentence.

There are things in the Bible that have been commonly overlooked. There are also things which are commonly believed to be in the Bible, but which are simply *not* there. The Bible speaks about being *"throughly* furnished unto all good works" (2 Tim. 3:17). It is easy to confuse "throughly" with "thoroughly." In this case, it does not make much difference in meaning. But sometimes just one letter *can* make quite a difference, like when a bum asked a Dunkard minister why he wore a beard. "I'm a Dunkard", the minister answered. "I'm a drunkard, too", said the bum, "but I shave now and then!"

Some make a similar mistake in reading Mark 16:1. It is not uncommon for people to add an "r" to the word "bought" which changes it to "brought" and the meaning of the whole verse can be affected! "And when the sabbath was past, Mary Magdalene, and Mary the mother of James, and Salome had BOUGHT [not brought] sweet spices, that they might come and anoint him."

The difference between "bought" and "brought" enters into the discussion regarding the time period between the burial and resurrection of Christ. Jesus spoke of this period as "three days and three nights" (Matt. 12:40). Though *tradition* is strong for the idea of Friday as the day of crucifixion, there are an increasing number of Christians who feel the crucifixion could have been as early as Wednesday, thus allowing time for a full three days *and* three nights. With this view, it is figured that there were *two* sabbaths that week—the high day sabbath (John 19:31) and the weekly sabbath—and a regular business day between during which the women *bought* their spices.

100

This would explain how it was *after* the sabbath they bought[1] their spices (Mk. 16:1) and prepared them. Then after preparing the spices, they rested on the sabbath (Lk. 23:56) before coming to the tomb on the first day of the week. It is not our purpose to lose the reader on this point, but these words have been necessary to point out how one letter can give an entirely different meaning to a verse.

The Bible does not mention a sycamore tree. The expression the Bible uses is "sycomore tree." Zacchaeus climbed up into a sycomore tree, for the Lord he wanted to see (Lk. 19:4). But whether sycamore or sycomore, the Bible tree was different than what most of us think of by this name. As its name implies in the Greek, the sycomore tree has characteristics of a fig tree and a mulberry tree. Its fruit is more like that of a fig tree, but its leaves are like a mulberry tree. The commentary by Barnes (p. 120) includes the following: "It not only bears several crops of figs during the year, but these figs grow on short stems along the trunk and large branches, and not at the end of twigs, as in other fruit-bearing trees" (see illustration).

Question: On which side of a house did the sycomore tree grow in Israel? Answer: On the outside.

NON-BIBLICAL QUOTATIONS

There are a number of quotations commonly supposed to be in the Bible but which are *not* there. A preacher who used the saying, "Cleanliness is next to godliness", said he had taken it from the Bible. Someone told him later, "You must have *taken* it from

---

1. The translators of our King James Version have used the expression "had bought", but the original is, simply, "the women bought spices." None of the translations I have checked have the word "had" at this place.

the Bible, it's not in there now!"

Actually, we know the quotation "Cleanliness is next to godliness" from a sermon given by John Wesley in 1740. His precise words were, "Clean is indeed next to godliness." Wesley put the words in quotation marks, a fact which may indicate this quotation had an earlier origin. Some believe it may go back as far as to the Hebrew father Phinehas ben Yair—over 2,000 years ago.

"God helps those who help themselves" probably appeared first in *Discourses Concerning Government* by Algernon Sidney, published in 1698. It is better-known from Benjamin Franklin's *Poor Richard's Almanac* for 1733 in which it was worded, "God helps him who helps himself."

"Each generation will grow wiser and weaker" is not found in the Bible. Its source is unknown, but it is probably based on the words of Walter Pope (1630-1714): "May I govern my passion with an absolute sway, and grow wiser and better, as my strength wears away."

Some believe the Bible says, "When in Rome do as the Romans do." This is not Biblical. Paul did say: "I am made all things to all men, that I might by all means save some" (1 Cor. 9:22), but this must be understood within its proper setting. The idea that a person in Rome should do as the Romans do could easily be carried to an unscriptural extreme!

"God works in mysterious ways his wonders to perform, he plants his footprints on the sea and rides upon the storm." These words are from a poem by William Cowper (1731-1800). It is true that God does work in ways that are mysterious to us. But this quotation is not in the Bible.

We should not make the mistake of saying the Bible says things it does not say. However, if a quotation is good, there is nothing wrong with using it—even though it is not in the Bible. When Paul was in Greece, he purposely quoted from some of their own poets to make a point as he spoke on Mars' hill. ". . . for in him we live, and move, and have our being; as certain of *your own poets have said*, For we are also his offspring" (Acts 17:28). From what Greek poetry was Paul quoting? The thought appears in the *Phaenomena* of Aratus and in the *Hymn to Zeus* of Cleanthes.

When writing to the Corinthians, Paul used the expression, "Evil communications corrupt good manners" (1 Cor. 15:33). This was quoted from Menander, an Athenian dramatist who lived from 342 to 291 B.C. In his *Thais*, which survives in fragmentary form, Menander said: "It must be that evil communications corrupt good manners." The saying had become proverbial and was used by Paul.

On another occasion, when writing to Titus, Paul apparently quoted from Epimenides (who lived in the sixth century B.C.) and was considered a prophet among the Cretians. "One of themselves, even a prophet of their own, said, The Cretians are always liars, evil beasts, slow bellies" (Titus 1:12).

Paul also used a quotation from Jesus which is of special interest in that it appears nowhere in the gospels. It may have been included in some early Christian writings which are no longer available or may have been passed down by word of mouth. Whatever the case, it was known as a saying of Jesus at the time of Paul, for he said: "Remember the words of the Lord Jesus, how he said, It is more blessed to give than to receive" (Acts 20:25). We know these words as the words of Jesus only because Paul quoted them here.

In the book of Jude, we are told that "Michael the archangel, when contending with the devil disputed about the body of Moses, durst not bring against him a railing accusation, but said, The Lord rebuke thee" (Jude 1:9). This information or quotation appears nowhere in the Old Testament. According to several of the early Christian fathers, including Clement of Alexandria and Origen, this information was from *The Assumption of Moses*, a Jewish apocyphal work of the first century A.D.

EXPRESSIONS SUGGESTED BY THE BIBLE

A number of present-day expressions—though not always exact quotations—were suggested by the Bible. "A little bird told me" may have come from Ecclesiastes 10:20: "For a bird of the air shall carry the voice, and that which hath wings shall tell the matter."

When speaking of certain doom upon an individual or country, we might say that "the handwriting is on the wall" which is based, of course, on the divine writing which announced the fall of Babylon (Daniel 5:5).

The expression "holier than thou" is commonly applied to people who profess to be more virtuous than others. This is found in Isaiah 65:5: "A people that provoketh me to anger . . . which say, Stand by thyself, come not near to me; for I am *holier than thou.*"

A person who barely escapes some calamity might say he escaped "by the skin of his teeth." This expression is based on Job 19:20: "I am escaped with the skin of my teeth."

The motto "In God We Trust" which appears on our money, though not an exact Biblical quotation, is based on verses such as Psalms 56:11: "In God have I put my trust."

HELPMATE. The Bible does not use the expression "helpmate." The reader will notice that a different expression is actually used in Genesis 2:18, "And the Lord God said, It is not good that the man should be alone; I will make him an *help meet* for him." The word "help" means helper and "meet" means suitable. Adam was given a helper suitable for him. At some point in the evolution of language, these two words became merged into help-meet, then helpmeet, and finally helpmate, as though meet and mate were the same! Consequently, today we have two words, helpmeet and helpmate, both of which are used interchangeably for a person's marriage partner.

MARRIAGE CEREMONY. There is no record in the Bible of a minister performing a marriage ceremony. The custom then was, and it is especially evident in the Old Testament, that the uniting of a couple was arranged by the heads of the two families involved. It was made legal by some exchange of goods or services.

Some might suppose the words of the marriage ceremony "for better or for worse, for richer or for poorer" are in the Bible. *Parade* magazine once ran a quiz that reflected this idea. One of the questions was: "How many wives does the Bible allow for each man?" The answer was: "Sixteen (four better, four worse, four richer, four poorer)"!

104

SAMSON. The accompanying illustration is from a famous painting by Andrea Mantegna (1431-1506) of Samson and Delilah as she is cutting his hair off. This reflects a common assumption: that Delilah cut off Samson's hair. This is not true. A *man* did it. "...and she called for a MAN, and she caused *him* to shave off the seven locks of his [Samson's] head" (Judges 16:19).

ABSALOM. It is commonly believed that Absalom got caught in an oak tree by the *hair* of his head. It is true that Absalom had long hair (2 Sam. 14:26) and this may be why some believe his hair became entangled in the branches while the mule he was riding went on. But this is what the Bible actually says: "And Absalom rode upon a mule, and the mule went under the thick boughs of a great oak, and his *head* caught hold of the oak, and he

105

was taken up between the heaven and the earth; and the mule that was under him went away" (2 Sam. 18:9-15). The word translated "head" is the normal word for a person's head. The word "hair" is an entirely different word. *Clarke's Commentary* (Vol. 2, p. 358) says: "It has been supposed that Absalom was caught by the *hair*, but no such thing is intimated in the text. Probably his neck was caught in the fork of a strong bough."

SEVEN HEAVENS. The Bible does not use the term "seven heavens." Though this expression may be found in the book of *Enoch* and in the writings of several religions, the Bible itself mentions only three heavens. "...caught up to the *third* heaven...caught up into paradise" (2 Cor. 12:2-4).

TREE. "As a tree falleth, so shall it lie" has become a popular phrase in evangelistic sermons, but it is not in the Bible (as such). The closest wording to this is Ecclesiastes 11:3: "If the tree fall toward the south, or toward the north, in the place where the tree falleth, there it shall be."

IMMORTAL SOUL. Though the words "soul" and "spirit" appear hundreds of times in the scriptures, never once does the Bible use the expression "immortal soul." The word "eternity" appears only once in the Bible and is applied to God—"the high and lofty One that inhabiteth eternity, whose name is Holy" (Isaiah 57:15). Psalms 111:9 says, "Holy and *reverend* is his name." This is the only time the word "reverend" appears in the Bible and it was applied, not to a preacher, but to God himself. The title was not applied to clergymen until the fifteenth century.

SERMON. The word "sermon" is not found in the Bible, though we commonly refer to Matthew, chapters 5-7, as the sermon on the mount.

REVELATIONS. The last book in the Bible is not the book of Revelations. There is no "s" on it. The correct title is given in verse 1: The Revelation of Jesus Christ.

GOLDEN RULE. The expression "golden rule" does not appear in the Bible nor do the words "Do unto others as you would have them do unto you"—not in this exact form. The thought is there, of course, as in Luke 6:31: "And as ye would that men should do to you, do ye also to them likewise." It should also be pointed out that this is not exclusively a New Testament thought. It is also in the Old Testament: "...thou shalt love thy neighbor as thyself" (Lev. 19:18).

PRIDE. Does the Bible say, "Pride goeth before a fall"? This would *seem* like a Biblical quotation, but what the Bible actually says is this: "Pride goeth before *destruction*, and a haughty spirit before a fall" (Proverbs 16:18).

MONEY. The Bible does not say that money is the root of all evil. Instead, "the *love* of money is the root of all evil" (1 Tim. 6:10). There is a difference.

WITCH. The phrase "the witch of Endor" does not occur in the text of the Bible. The Bible simply mentions "a woman that hath a familiar spirit at Endor" (1 Sam. 28:7). Some believe she was a *medium* rather than a witch.

PRODIGAL SON. The term "prodigal son" does not appear in the Bible text, though the word "prodigal", meaning wasteful, fits the path followed by the wayward son (Lk. 15:11-32).

GOOD SAMARITAN. We use the term "the good Samaritan"—but the actual wording in the Bible is this: "A certain Samaritan...had compassion" (Lk. 10:33). He had compassion on the man that Jesus said "went down from Jerusalem to Jericho" (verse 30). Any who have traveled this Jericho road know that the word "down" in this verse should be taken as just that. Jerusalem is about 2,581 feet above sea level and Jericho is 825 feet *below* sea level. So in the trip of 23 miles from Jerusalem to Jericho, the road drops almost 3,500 feet!

PARABLES. It is commonly supposed that Jesus used parables in order to make the meaning of his message clear. This may have been true of *some* parables, but it is certainly not true of all of them. To the contrary, Jesus spoke in parables so that the crowd would *not* see his point and would *not* understand: "And his disciples asked him, saying, What might this parable be? And he said, Unto *you* it is given to know the mysteries of the kingdom of God: but to others in parables; that seeing they might not *see, and hearing they might not* understand" (Lk. 8:9, 10).

SMILE. Some say that Jesus never smiled. I don't believe this.

The scriptures do refer to him as "a man of sorrows and acquainted with grief" (Isaiah 53:3). But we must also remember that he was anointed with the oil of *gladness* above his fellows (Heb. 1:9).

CHRISTMAS. The word "Christmas", of course, does not appear in the Bible. Even though Christmas is celebrated on December 25, most now realize that this date is incorrect. The fact that the shepherds were out watching their flocks at the time of Christ's birth (Lk. 2:8) strongly indicates that it was not during the middle of winter.

MANGER. The Bible does not say Jesus was born in a manger. "And she [Mary] brought forth her firstborn son, and wrapped him in swaddling clothes, and *laid him in a manger*; because there was no room for them in the inn" (Lk. 2:7). The word manger comes from a verb meaning "to eat" and means here literally a "feeding-place."

The Bible does not use the word "stable" in connection with the birth of Jesus. Some have pictured the place of his birth as resembling a barn on a typical American farm. But the area in which a manger was located by an inn for travelers was probably only a very primitive and simple shelter in which animals used for travel could be fed and kept overnight.

MANGER SCENES. "Manger scenes" are commonly displayed in which not only the shepherds, but the *wisemen* also, are pictured as being present. The shepherds did come to the manger, but not the wisemen. It was later that the wisemen came, and not to the manger, but to a *house* (Matt. 2:11).

We do not want to overmake a point like this, but such can serve to show how people have believed things to be Biblical which are actually only traditions of men. We are reminded of a woman who went to see the movie *The Ten Commandments*. She claimed the movie made the Bible so real to her and that she "never knew what Moses looked like until she saw the movie"!

THREE WISEMEN. The Bible does not say there were *three* wisemen. A tradition says they were three kings: Gasper, Melchoir, and Balthasar. A song goes: "We three kings of Orient are, bearing gifts, we traverse afar." The fact that they offered

108

gifts of gold, frankincense, and myrrh (Matt. 2:11) does not, necessarily, prove there were only three of them. Nor does the Bible refer to them as kings.

Many scholars believe these men were Magi, members of a priestly caste in Persia. In Palestine, the "east" commonly referred to Persia; and the religion of the Magi included a belief in the coming of a Messiah. Some translations use the term astrologers. But whatever may be implied by the designation "wise men," as has been said, we know they were *wise* because they were seeking Jesus.

VIRGIN BIRTH. Many suppose the term "virgin birth" is in the Bible. But this expression is not found in the King James Version, the Revised Version, or any other version. The scriptures teach that the birth of Jesus was the *result* of a miracle—being the son of God and without an earthly father (Lk. 1:30-35)—yet the emphasis is not put so much on his *birth* as being miraculous, but on his *conception*. The real miracle took place nine months before his birth.

Believing that Jesus was supernaturally conceived is not the same as a Romish belief which would make his birth such that he passed from Mary's body by a miracle—as after the resurrection he passed through closed doors—thus leaving her physical parts intact. Then, according to the belief, Joseph kept her as a virgin all her life and that now in heaven she is the blessed virgin, queen

of heaven. This is known as the doctrine of the "perpetual virginity." But the Biblical explanation is that Joseph "knew her not *till* she had brought forth her first-born son" (Matt. 1:25). The idea of the *perpetual* virginity of Mary is not even hinted at in the scriptures.

TRINITY. The word "trinity" is not in the Bible. Artists have had their difficulties trying to depict the Trinity, as can be seen in the drawing of a window of the sixteenth century in

109

the church of Notre Dame at Chalons, France. The Bible speaks of the Father, Son, and Holy Ghost, but the expression "God the Father, God the Son, and God the Holy Ghost" does not appear in this form. Though Jesus is referred to as "God" in the scriptures (John 1:1; Hebrews 1:8), he is most often called "the son of God" (Mk. 1:1, Acts 8:37, Heb. 4:14, etc.)

BAPTISM OF THE HOLY SPIRIT. The expression "baptism *of* the Holy Spirit" is commonly used, but this is not the actual Bible wording. Instead of using the word "of", the Bible says the disciples were "baptized *with* the Holy Ghost", were "filled *with* the Holy Ghost" (Acts 1:5, 2:4), the Spirit was "poured out" or "fell" upon them (Acts 2:17, 10:44-48). Such terms are used interchangeably as the New Testament repeatedly stresses the Spirit-filled life.

TEMPLE. The term "holy of holies" is commonly used to designate the most holy place in the ancient temple. But the expression, in this form, does not appear in the Bible.

RAPTURE. The word "rapture" comes from the word *rapere*, meaning to seize. It is the same word, incidently, from which the word "rape" is taken. The term "rapture" does not appear in the Bible, but is now commonly applied to the statement of Paul that believers will be "caught up . . . in the clouds, to meet the Lord in the air" (1 Thess. 4:17).

MILLENNIUM. The word "millennium" does not appear in the Bible, but the word means "one thousand" and Revelation 20 does mention "a thousand years."

Because we have pointed out these numerous expressions and words which are not in the Bible, we do not mean to imply, necessarily, that their use is wrong. We should not put ourselves in a spiritual strait jacket. After all, the word BIBLE is not in the Bible either! Some of the terms we have mentioned do indeed represent scriptural ideas; quite a few do not. But these are technical points and may be of interest only to the advanced Bible student.

We should not make the mistake of believing that a precise knowledge of doctrinal points is any indication of true spirituality. We do not encourage people to play "doctrinal detective" so that in hearing a message they only hear the fine points on which they may not totally agree. We must avoid a critical and negative attitude. We must not major on minors. If truth has come to us, we should rejoice in that truth, and seek to be humble and loving, bearing in mind that "knowledge puffeth up, but love edifieth" (1 Cor. 8:1).

*　*　*　*　*

One man who prayed for patience said this: "God give me patience and give it to me NOW!"

*　*　*　*　*

If there's a hypocrite standing between you and God...he's closer to God than you are!

*　*　*　*　*

This fellow came rushing up to a man on the street and asked: "Do you want to be a Jehovah's Witness?" He told him he was sorry, he couldn't; he didn't even see the accident.

*　*　*　*　*

Marriage should be to "have and to *hold*," not to have and to *scold*.

*　*　*　*　*

When God made the first human pair, he made them male and female. It was Adam and Eve—not Adam and Steve.

*　*　*　*　*

Some people are so heavenly minded they are no earthly good.

*　*　*　*　*

Merely going to a church does not make a man a Christian any more than going to a garage makes him a Dodge.

Chapter 9

THE BIBLE—USED AND MISUSED

Many people seek divine guidance by opening the Bible and placing their finger on a verse at random. But this practice did not originate with the Bible. The Greeks used verses taken from the *Iliad* and the *Odyssey*. The Romans used Virgil's *Aeneid* and the Mohammedans, the *Koran*.

We have no example or instruction within the Bible for choosing a verse at random. I am not saying it is wrong, but such could easily be carried to a superstitious extreme, as though the Bible were some type of glorified Ouija board.

I have seen people open the Bible for "guidance" and then try again if they did not get a verse that fit in some way the situation at hand. It is not uncommon for them to get into the "begats" or something entirely irrelevant. Other times, a verse might seem to fit a situation. A young lady who was going with a huge and somewhat uncouth young man wondered if she should marry him. When she let the Bible fall open for guidance, she read this verse: "The Lord that delivered me out of the paw of the lion, and out of the paw of the bear, he will deliver me out of the hand of this *Philistine*" (1 Sam. 17:37), the reference being to Goliath. But affection proved stronger than superstition and she married him anyhow, with no regrets.

The tale is sometimes told of a man who opened the Bible for guidance and put his finger on the verse that said: "Judas went and hanged himself." He opened again and it said: "Go and do thou likewise." When he tried again, he read: "What thou doest, do quickly", and finally, "And as many as do these things shall inherit eternal life"!

By taking only part of what the Bible says, one could even prove "there is no God" (Psalms 53:1). But when we take all of the verse, we discover it is "the *fool* that hath said in his heart, There is no God."

A young couple when first married used to share in doing the evening dishes. She would wash the dishes, he would wipe them. After a while the man grew tired with this little chore and asked

112

to be dismissed. Besides, he felt that wiping dishes wasn't man's work anyhow. But the woman found a verse in the Bible which, she felt, proved otherwise: "And I will wipe Jerusalem as a MAN wipeth a dish, wiping it, and turning it upside down" (2 Kings 21:13).

A woman who did not want to get up early in the morning used the scripture: "Woe unto them that rise up early in the morning" (Isaiah 5:11). But when we read the *rest* of the verse, it has an entirely different meaning: "Woe unto them that rise up early in the morning, that they may follow strong drink; that continue until night, till wine inflame them"! The setting is that of drunken revelling and failure to regard the work of the Lord. It has nothing to do with what time a person gets up in the morning under other circumstances.

I am reminded of a preacher I heard a few years ago who was an early riser. "I beat my wife up almost every morning", he said. Some misunderstood this and thought he was *mean* to his wife!

Jesus said that man should live "by *every* word of God" (Matt. 4:4). An overall, consistent study of *everything* the Bible says on a subject is far more sound than basing conclusions on a single verse taken at random or otherwise.

PRAY WITHOUT CEASING?

The Bible says, "Pray without ceasing" (1 Thess. 5:17). Taking this verse *alone*, some suppose we should pray all the time; should never stop praying; should always be in an attitude of prayer. The fact is, no one has ever done this. Even Jesus ceased to pray. "As he was praying in a certain place, when he CEASED . . ." (Luke 11:1).

Let us suppose we met a man we hadn't seen for five years and made the following statement: "I *haven't stopped* praying for you; I *always* remember you in prayer." He would not take this to mean that every minute of every day for five years we had been praying for him. He would understand that from time to time we had continued to pray for him. It was in this same sense that Paul said we should pray "without ceasing."

This point becomes clear when we notice how Paul used the expression in *other* verses. In writing to the Romans he said: "Without ceasing I make mention of you always in my prayers" (Rom. 1:9). To the Colossians he said: "We do not cease to pray for you" (Col. 1:9). To the Ephesians he wrote: "I cease not to mention you in my prayers" (Eph. 1:16). To Timothy he wrote: "Without ceasing I have remembrance of thee in my prayers" (2 Tim. 1:3).

Now, if "without ceasing" meant to pray and never stop praying in the absolute sense, and if Paul prayed without ceasing for the Romans, he would have had no time to pray for the Colossians or the others he mentioned! It is evident that to pray "without ceasing" speaks of consistent and faithful prayer. It is not a command to do the impossible.

JUDGES—THOSE LEAST ESTEEMED?

Some believe that Paul instructed the Corinthians to "set them to judge who are least esteemed in the church" (1 Cor. 6:4). The fact is, Paul was *not* telling them to set someone least esteemed to judge. This is what *they* were doing. "Ye . . . set them to judge who are least esteemed in the church." The very next sentence clarifies the whole thing: "*I speak this to your shame*"!

If Paul was telling them to set people least esteemed to judge, who would decide who was least esteemed in the church? The scriptures teach that we are to esteem other believers highly (Phil. 2:3; 1 Thess. 5:13).

The Goodspeed translation shows the point that Paul was making: "If then you have ordinary matters to be settled, will you submit them for judgment to men who are nothing in the church? *I ask it to shame you.* Has it come to this, that there is not a single wise man among you who could settle a disagreement between one brother and another, but one Christian has to go to law with another, and before unbelievers too?"

When this portion is studied in context, it is clear that Paul was not instructing the Corinthians to set those least esteemed by the church to judge.

Sometimes gospel songs—though beautiful and often expressing a good thought—have been based on a verse out of context. Millions have heard the song made famous by Roy Acuff, *The Great Speckled Bird*. It has a haunting melody. The title is based on Jeremiah 12:9: "Mine heritage is unto me as a *speckled bird*, the birds round about are against her." In the song, the bird represents the church, which, having a high standard, is despised by others. But when God's heritage was likened to a "speckled bird" in the Bible, it was not used in a good sense. It had corrupted the worship of God with heathenish rites, had become like a lion roaring against God, so he *hated* it (verse 8)!

Another song says: "Lord build me a cabin in the corner of glory-land, in the shade of the tree of life that it may ever stand..." The writer had a good thought, but these words do not line up with the Biblical text. The tree of life is mentioned as being "in the *midst* of the paradise of God" (Rev. 2:7). If the cabin was built in the shade of this tree, it would have to be in the *center*—not the *corner*—of glory-land.

PANAMA CANAL

It is said that when they first began to plan the Panama Canal, some felt it was against the Bible to build a canal between North and South America. The scripture that was used was this: "What God hath joined together, let not man put asunder" (Matt. 19:6). This was really taking a text out of context!

It is commonly supposed that the canal (which shortened the voyage between Atlantic and Pacific ports by as much as 7,000 miles) crosses Panama *from east to west*. But from Limon Bay to Gatun Lake, the canal runs due south, then takes a turn eastward so that the Pacific side is actually more than twenty miles *east* of its Atlantic beginning!

Not only have verses been used out of context, some ideas have even been built on *part* of a word! One article I read attempted to link "Gog and Magog" (Ezekiel 38) with Jews—Russian Jews! What was the proof text? Revelation 2:9: "I know the blasphemy of them which say they are Jews, and are not, but are the synaGOGue of Satan"! Notice the word "Gog" appears in the word synagogue!

This reminds me of some who teach that when the Bible says

Jerusalem it really means the United States of America because the letters U.S.A. appear in the word JerUSAlem!

Some go to great lengths to find the United States in the Bible. Some years ago I read material which quoted Joshua 21:41 which mentions the number 48: "And the cities of the Levites within the possession of the children of Israel were forty and eight cities." An attempt was made to link this verse with the United States because there were, at that time, 48 states! Now, of course, with the annexation of Hawaii and Alaska, there are fifty states. With this, the little theory built around the number 48 became obsolete.

THE AMERICAN FLAG

In 1961 I attended a meeting in San Diego, California, in which a fairly well-known minister spoke along the lines of healing and faith. At the close of the message, he asked if there were any questions. One lady stood and asked: "Brother -------, don't you think the United States has committed a horrible sin in changing our flag from 48 stripes to 50 stripes since we took in Alaska and Hawaii? Jesus took 48 stripes upon his back and this was symbolized by the 48 stripes on the American flag. Now this has been changed!"

The speaker was careful not to put the woman down for the gross ignorance displayed in her question and statement. He merely pointed out that we are not told exactly how many stripes were placed upon the back of Christ. According to the laws of the Jews, not more than 40 stripes were to be inflicted (Deut. 25:3). But the number of stripes inflicted upon the back of Christ has nothing to do with the American flag!

There never were 48 stripes on the American flag. The stripes on the flag were not changed when Alaska and Hawaii were granted statehood in 1959-1960. It was the number of *stars* that was changed from 48 to 50.

SPIRITUAL GIFTS

One night while speaking at a church in Nevada, I mentioned the nine gifts of the Spirit that are listed in First Corinthians 12:8-10. After the service someone came to me and told me there

were *ten* gifts of the Spirit. This was a new one to me! The proof for this, I was told, could be found in Genesis 24:10: when Abraham's servant went to seek a wife for Isaac, he didn't take nine camels, he took TEN! I still haven't been able to figure out the connection.

TOWER OF BABEL

One Minister whose writings have had a wide circulation for

quite a few years, teaches that there were 600,000 men employed in the building of the tower of Babel. He states that it was about 60 miles around its base and that when it was destroyed, it was 3,650 MILES high (this is not a misprint!). When it fell, he says, it fell with such force that it broke the earth into continents and islands as it is today! The scripture that was quoted is Genesis 10:25: "In the days of Peleg the earth was divided." The way the article was written, if one didn't know better, he could easily assume that this information could all be found somewhere in the Bible.

It was only a month or so after I read these things (back in 1960) that I happened to meet this man on a train. I asked him the basis for these things. He said much of this knowledge came to him "by revelation." The reader may judge for himself the feasibility of a tower in ancient times being 3,650 miles high.

A FLAT EARTH?

When Columbus sought to establish that the earth is round, he met much opposition. He was told that his idea was against the Bible. Besides, if the earth was round, and he sailed down under, "the rotundity of the earth would present a kind of mountain up which it would be impossible for him to sail, even with the fairest wind."

Church fathers such as Lactantius, Eusiebius of Caesarea, Jerome, Chrysostom, and Augustine all thought the earth was flat, a surface bordered by waters, and upon which the dome of the sky rested. In 535 A.D., Cosmas of Alexandria wrote *Christian Topography*, a book which became a standard for centuries. If the earth was not flat, the book argued, how could men on the other side of the globe see the Lord descending through the air at his second coming!

Even in more recent times, the idea that the earth is flat has been held by a few. This was taught by John Alexander Dowie, founder of Zion City, Illinois, and famous preacher at the turn of the century. His successor, Wilbur Glenn Voliva, offered $5,000 to anyone who could prove to his satisfaction that the earth was round. At his death in 1942, he had not paid out the money. His successor, M. J. Mintern, also insisted that the earth is flat. In 1948, photographs were taken from rockets 57 miles above the White Sands proving grounds in New Mexico. The curve of the earth's surface was evident. These photographs were shown to Mintern, but he was unimpressed. "When you have something really worth-while in the way of proof that the earth is spherical", he said, "let me know" (*The New York Times*, October 23, 1948).

The first letter of every continent's name is the same as the last—AmericA, AntarcticA, EuropE, AsiA, AustraliA, and AfricA.

Years ago when there was talk about how someday it might be possible for man to go to the moon, some said that God would never allow it, that it was contrary to the Bible. (The tower of Babel was mentioned.) However, there was actually nothing in the Bible to indicate that men would not go to the moon. We have lived to see this actually happen, though there are some who suppose it was a gigantic hoax performed on a sound stage at Disneyland.

Believing that God carried out his judgments by using lightning, some churchmen in Massachusetts argued that Benjamin Franklin's invention of the lightning rod was an attempt to offset the intentions of the Almighty. They felt the use of lightning rods had angered the Lord and that is why he sent the earthquake of 1755.

ELECTRICITY—SATAN'S SPIRIT?

A few years ago I read an article which set forth the belief that lightning or electricity is the spirit of Satan, just as the Holy Spirit is the Spirit of God! Luke 10:19 was quoted: "I beheld Satan as *lightning* fall from heaven"! Revelation 9:1 was also worked into the theory: "And to him was given the *key* to the bottomless pit." This was taken to refer to Benjamin Franklin, the "key" being the key that he tied to a kite when experimenting with electricity. The verses that follow speak about the air being darkened. These were taken as references to modern factories, most of which were made possible through electricity to run machinery, lights, etc. The writer was opposed to modern inventions. Yet, the inconsistency is apparent, for it was an electrically operated printing press that printed his article that said electricity was the spirit of the Devil. Oh, well.

There was a time when some objected to street lights. It was argued that people would stay out all night and catch cold. Some even claimed it was wrong on Biblical grounds—after all, God had divided the light from the darkness (Gen. 1:18) and to interfere in any way with this order was wrong!

A practice that has become quite widespread in this century is "daylight-saving time." This sets the clock ahead one hour for several months so that there is an additional hour of daylight in the evening (as it were). I have heard it said, on at least one occasion, that this is "against the Bible"—that *somewhere* in the Bible it said the Devil would change the times and seasons in the last days! (Daniel 7:25?).

On the other hand, someone in favor of daylight-saving time could quote the scripture which says: "It shall come to pass, that at evening time it shall be light" (Zech. 14:7), but neither text has any connection with daylight-saving time.

A preacher was informed by an obstetrician that his wife could be delivered of their child only by Caesarean section. He refused to grant permission because of God's pronouncement to Eve that in *pain* women were to bring forth children. The result was that his wife died. He soon married again—but he was sure he had kept the *letter* of the scripture.

It is widely supposed that the pronouncement to Eve in Genesis says that in *pain* women would bring forth children, but what Genesis 3:16 actually says is this: ". . .in *sorrow* thou shalt bring forth children." Judgment was also pronounced on Adam— the ground was cursed with thorns and thistles. He would experience difficulties in working the soil and obtaining food from it. In the sweat of his face would he eat bread. To deny the available help to a woman in childbirth—because of the pronouncement to Eve—would be just as silly as to say that a farmer should not have a *tractor* to plow his field, because God cursed the ground for Adam. By the same reasoning, a person should not have air conditioning, since God wanted man to sweat; and since God wanted man to sweat, man should not hinder it by using deodorant!

WAITING ON MINISTRY?

If verses are taken out of context, people can find Biblical statements to fit almost any situation or provide an excuse. I knew a man once who hardly ever worked. His family lived in poverty. He told me he was called to serve God, that his ministry had not developed yet, but he was "waiting" on his ministry. He quoted Romans 12:7. But does this verse about "waiting" on one's ministry mean to do nothing? No, just the opposite!

Here is what the passage says: "Having then gifts differing according to the grace that is given to us, whether prophecy, let us prophesy according to the proportion of faith; or ministry, *let us wait on our ministering*: or he that teacheth on teaching; or he that exhorteth, on exhortation" (Rom. 12:6-8).

The simple meaning is that if one is called to prophesy, let him prophesy. If one is called to minister, let him minister. If one is called to teach, let him teach. If one is called to exhort, let him exhort. In other words, what one is called to do, *let him do it*. When the King James translators put the words "let us wait", they never intended to convey the idea of waiting a period of time. By waiting on one's ministry, the intended meaning is that one would do what he was called to do, to serve in that capacity. It should be understood in the same sense as a waiter in a restaurant waits on tables. His "waiting" does not mean he is to stand around and do nothing. He does his job.

If a church is growing and prospering, some say in effect: "Look at us. We are growing. We are getting the job done. We are the ones God is blessing. We must be the true church!" Others that have only a few people and seem only one step from failure quote the scripture which says: "Fear not little flock", with the emphasis on the word *little*!

One preacher told me he wasn't upset about the small attendance in his church. "The Bible says that only a few are saved anyhow", he reasoned. "We already have a few, so why try to get more?" Another preacher told me once that if he tried to get any more members, he might get troublemakers, these might split his church, and the latter end would be worse than the first!

PROPHECY EXPERTS?

In an effort to link world events with verses in the Bible, some prophetic teachers have been guilty of taking verses entirely out

121

of their proper setting to make a point. Some years ago a prophetic ministry taught that Mussolini would be the Antichrist. Even Isaiah 14:11, "...the noise of thy *viols*", was quoted as though it referred to Mussolini playing his *violin*!

Others tried to link Hitler with certain scriptures. When reports came of his death, some felt this could not be. I can remember articles years ago which stated that Hitler wasn't really dead, that he was re-organizing his forces in South America, to finally appear with a revived Germany. But as of this year (1979), Hitler would be 90 years old. At this age, he hardly seems a likely candidate for world dictator!

Some tried to link John F. Kennedy with the prophecy concerning the "Beast" of Revelation 13. When he was assassinated, it was pointed out that the beast would be wounded in the head (Rev. 13:3). In the Biblical symbolism, however, it was only one head of a many-headed beast that was wounded; and that, not with a gun, but a *sword* (Rev. 13:14). Perhaps Kennedy isn't really dead at all—some reasoned. Perhaps he is still in Dallas being kept alive by doctors in a secret room of Parkland Hospital, for Revelation 13:3 says, "...his deadly wound was healed." What novel ideas some try to read into the Bible!

In order to keep records of contributions that are made, some churches use a system in which each member is assigned a number and offering envelopes which have this number printed on them. I know a man who insisted that no one was about to give him a *number*. He not only quit contributing to his church, he also quit the church! His strong opposition about being given a number was based—supposedly—on Revelation 13:18: "Let him that hath understanding count the number of the beast...his number is six hundred threescore and six." But what could this possibly have to do with offering envelopes?

If someone thinks being given a number is the mark of the beast, then everyone has the mark! In order to receive mail, we have an address number (street or box) as well as a zip code number. We have a telephone number and an area code number. We have a social security number. Code numbers appear on almost every canned or packaged good we use. The license plate on our car has a number and there is a number on our driver's license. Numbers appear on our money, as well as on checks and credit cards. Even the Bible is divided into chapters and verses which can be located by referring to certain numbers. Numbers are everywhere. Only a person given to gross superstition would think numbers are evil.

A young minister told me about a lady who quit his church because she discovered his car license had three sixes on it. She figured the minister was cursed! I received a letter once that expressed the view that a church in a certain city was under a curse because its phone number happened to be listed on page 666 of the telephone directory!

BAPTISMAL FORMULA

As you know, some churches baptize using the titles "Father, Son, and Holy Ghost" (Matt. 28:19), while others believe that baptism should be in the name of the Lord Jesus Christ (Acts 2:38). This has been often debated among certain groups. In his zeal to oppose using the titles "Father, Son, and Holy Ghost", one man said that anyone that was baptized this way had taken the mark of the beast! What was the proof? Well, if you add up the letters in the words "Father", "Son", and "Holy Ghost", there are 18 letters. Divide this by three and it averages six letters for each title. By placing these three sixes side-by-side, we get 666. The folly of such methods of interpretation should be apparent to all.

On the other hand, a man who opposed baptism in the name of Jesus Christ, carried his view to another extreme. This man told me—in all seriousness—that Peter *made a mistake* on the day of Pentecost when he told the people to be baptized in the name of Jesus Christ! His words went something like this: "Jesus said to baptize in the name of the Father, Son, and Holy Ghost. But Peter *disobeyed* and told people to be baptized in the name of Jesus Christ. The church had just gotten started and apostasy was already setting in! I would rather believe what Jesus said than what Peter said."

Personally, we do not believe Peter made a mistake on the day of Pentecost, nor do we believe there is any contradition between Matthew 28:19 and Acts 2:38.

After speaking at a church service one night, a lady asked me if

I knew the verse in which the cigarette was mentioned in the Bible. "Is it the one in which Rebekah lighted off her camel?", I asked. This was not the one. Instead, she pointed out Proverbs 16:27: "An ungodly man diggeth up evil: and *in his lips there is as a burning fire.*"

A look at the *context*, however, indicates that the reference pertains to sins of the mouth or tongue such as *gossip*. It was a similar figure of speech used by James in the New Testament. "The tongue is a little member, and boasteth great things...the tongue is a *fire*, a world of iniquity...it setteth on fire the course of nature; and it is set on fire of hell" (James 3:5, 6).

Cigarettes are not mentioned in the Bible. They were not in use or known in the area and at the time the Bible was being written. Europeans probably first learned of smoking when it was observed in the West Indies by the crew of Columbus in 1492. A pipe, the *tobago* (from which the word "tobacco" is derived) was in use and the cigarette (or whatever it was called at that time among the natives) was made with thin palm bark to hold the tobacco and smoked through the *nose*. It was not until the end of the seventeenth century that smoking became known and practiced world-wide.

At one time, the tobacco plant was believed to have extraordinary healing powers. In 1559 the French ambassador to Portugal, Jean Nicot, sent seeds to his queen, Catherine de Medicis. For this service, Nicot's name has lived on in the Latin botanical name for tobacco, *nicotiana*, and in our word *nicotine*.

I agree with the Surgeon General's report: Cigarette smoking is dangerous to your health.

Some pray: "Lord, take my cigarettes, take my cigarettes". But the Lord doesn't smoke! Why would he take someone's cigarettes? Certainly I believe in God's power to help people obtain victory over habits or problems. But a lot of time people are telling God to do this or that, and they refuse to do *their* part. We can pray, "Lord, I want a close walk with you." Fine. But the Bible says: "Draw nigh to God, and he will draw nigh to you" (James 4:8). There are some things God wants *us* to do.

Some people said to their minister: "Why are you preaching so hard at us, we haven't done anything!" To this he replied: *"That's the trouble!"* The Lord spoke to Ezekiel about people like that. "They come unto thee as the people cometh, and they sit before thee as my people, and they *hear* thy words, but they will not DO them...thou art unto them as a very lovely song of one that hath a pleasant voice, and can play well on an instrument: for they *hear* thy words, but they DO THEM NOT" (Ezekiel 33:31, 32).

In this time when many are cold and a few are frozen (spiritually), may God help us to be *"doers* of the word, and not hearers only"* (James 1:22).

*　　*　　*　　*　　*

Some folks are like a lady who stood in church and testified, "I love everybody I see," but she had her eyes shut the whole time.

*　　*　　*　　*　　*

There is an ancient story about a man who wanted to find the true God. He collected a bunch of idols and put them in a sack. As he walked down the street he tripped and all the little gods were broken except one. He figured this one must be the true God. He set it up and began to worship it. Then a cat came along and knocked it over. So he figured the cat must be God. But then a dog came along and chased the cat off. So he worshiped the dog. When his wife saw him worshiping the dog, she threw a broom at the dog and it fled. Then he decided his wife must be God. He put her upon a pedestal and began to worship her. Being overcome with this attention, she began to faint. As she fell into his arms, she said, "Oh my Lord!" The man thought she was talking about him, so he concluded that *he* must be God! It is a fact, the "God" many people serve is *self*.

Chapter 10

FREEDOM FROM FEAR
AND OTHER MESSAGES

"God hath not given us the spirit of FEAR" (2 Timothy 1:7).

"FEAR hath torment" (1 John 4:18).

"God is love...perfect love casteth out FEAR" (1 John 4:16, 18).

Timothy, a young preacher, had apparently allowed fear to hinder his ministry. It was for this reason that Paul wrote to him exhorting him to "stir up the gift of God" within him—not to let fear hold him back—"FOR God hath not given us the spirit of fear." If our motives are right, we should never let fear stand in our way. Some never try to do anything for God—to exercise a ministry—because they are afraid they will fail. But if they don't try, they have FAILED ALREADY. Fear brings defeat instead of victory, failure instead of success. God has not given us the spirit of fear.

Jesus repeatedly taught that we should not fear, should not worry, should not be of a fearful mind. His message was *for* FAITH and *against* FEAR. He spoke in parables about how fear hinders, of a man who was afraid to use this talent and who lost, consequently, even that which he had. Yet, tragically, we see many followers of Jesus today troubled with fear. This should not be!

SUPERSTITIOUS FEARS

Many things that people worry about are things which will never happen. They are *superstitious* fears. One night when I was a boy, probably about five years of age, I was putting a picture puzzle together. It was a picture of a dog who had undone a ball of yarn. While working on this puzzle, a house up the street from us caught on fire. I remember the bright lights of the fire trucks, the crowd that gathered, and the flames shooting up into the sky! The damage to the house was actually not too great, no one was hurt, and it was soon repaired. But to a child, the scene that night was frightening. A seed of fear was planted in my mind. For some

126

reason, I never wanted to put that particular puzzle together again! Why? Did I suppose there was a connection? Did I think that if I worked that puzzle again another fire might start? Of course this was only a childish experience, but even as grownups, do we not also sometimes harbor unnecessary fears?

A few years ago, we were traveling through Los Angeles and stopped to eat at a place called Arby's (Arby's is one of the fast food chains—like McDonald's—only it specializes in roast beef sandwiches.) When we got back into the car, the car would not start. First we supposed it was battery trouble, but the car would not start even with jumper cables. Then we assumed it was the starter that was bad. But the trouble was more serious. It ended up a friend of ours came the next day and we towed the car home—quite a distance—to our mechanic to be worked on. To make a long story short, this car trouble involved a lot of inconvenience and expense.

Then about two weeks later, we were traveling near Sacramento and got off the freeway to get something quick to eat. Well, at that particular exit, we discovered the only place to eat was another Arby's! You can imagine what thoughts went through our minds. None of us said anything at first—but I suppose we were all *thinking* it! Superstition might have directed to go somewhere else, but we were in a hurry. As I parked the car at Arby's, Ralph K. (our son then age 10) asked if I was going to turn the car off—perhaps I should leave the motor running! I turned it off, assuring him there was no connection between the other trouble and this. When we came back out, what do you suppose happened? Why the car started *just fine*. Obviously there was no connection between this Arby's and another Arby's 400 miles away! Yet, perhaps superstitiously, in the back of our minds was there not a tiny fear?

There is a highway which begins in southern Arizona, runs north through part of New Mexico and into Colorado. It is numbered Highway 666. There are actually people who would rather not drive this highway because of the number. I know people who feel they should drive very carefully while on this road! Of course it is always sound judgment to drive carefully, but why on Highway 666 any more than Highway 66 or any other? Obviously highway 666 has nothing to do with the mention of 666 in Revelation 13. Two entirely different things are in view, the only similarity being the number. Yet often *supersition* causes people to worry about things which have no real basis.

Superstition dies hard. Some still fear bad luck if they break a mirror, especially if it happens on Friday the 13th! Some buildings that have many floors will omit floor 13; that is, the floors are numbered up to 12, then the next is 14, etc. Some people simply would not feel comfortable in an apartment or office on floor number 13! Sometimes hospitals will not have a room 13. Others, while they know certain things are only superstition, would not want to walk under a ladder or have a black cat cross their path—just in case!

But even in things more serious—I am not saying there are not *real* problems in life!—God can give peace in the place of fear. "God is our refuge and strength, a very present help in trouble. Therefore will not we FEAR, though the earth be removed, and though the mountains be carried into the midst of the sea" (Ps. 46:1, 2). A similar thought has been expressed in a present-day spiritual by Doris Akers,

This old world may toss and tumble; this old world may rock and roll.
The sun above may turn to ashes and all fury may unfold,
Every star may fall from heaven, and the earth may take a stroll,
But the Lord will never leave me, he's the lover of my soul!

Or, as Stuart Hamblin has expressed it in one of his songs,

Should the sun and the moon in time flicker and die,
And the earth wander off like a tramp through the sky,
The darkness can't hide me, He''ll find me I know,
For men are his diamonds and he loves me so.

Hebrews 13:5, 6 says: "...for he hath said, I will never leave thee, nor forsake thee. So that we may boldly say, The Lord is my helper, and I will not FEAR what man shall do unto me." Even in the "valley of the shadow of death", he has promised to be with us, and even there we shall "FEAR no evil" (Psalm 23). "In *all* these things we are *more than conquerors* through him" (Romans 8:37).

WINCHESTER HOUSE

The accompanying photograph (used by permission) is an aerial

view of the south side of the famous Winchester Mystery House, San Jose, California. A fortune had come to Mrs. Sarah Winchester—royalties of $1,000 a day—from her husband's firearms company. For 38 years Mrs. Winchester had crews working day and night who kept adding on to her house—more rooms, secret passsages, and trap doors! One cupboard door opens to a storage space of one-half inch, while the closet directly across from it opens to the back 30 rooms of the sprawling home! Several stairways lead nowhere. The house features hundreds of doors, 47 fireplaces, 52 skylights, and over 10,000 windows.

Why did Mrs. Winchester keep building? Because of FEAR. A spiritualist medium had told her that as long as there was the sound of hammers and construction continued on her house, she would not die! The Bible speaks of some who because of "FEAR of death" spend their whole lifetime in *bondage* (Heb. 2:15).

Often one worry leads to another. What if this were to happen?—and if this happened, then what about that?—and if that happened...... It is an endless curse. Perhaps you have heard the slogan: "Why worry when you can pray?" Some have changed this around and say: "Why pray when you can worry?" It is reverse psychology, but it makes a point. The point is that *worry does no good*. Sometimes, in fact, the worry becomes more traumatic than the problem itself. In a famous speech, Franklin Roosevelt said: "The only thing we need to fear is FEAR itself."

The words of Job have been often quoted: "For the thing which I greatly *feared* is come upon me" (Job 3:25). Job had a fear of certain things—and they happened to him. But this is not *always* the case. There have been millions of people who have feared things people worry about which never happened to them! Many go through life with fear of a dread disease—and never get it. Others live in fear that they will get in a car wreck—and never do. What good does this worrying do? Most things people worry about never happen! This very fact may help us not to worry. And, if something *is* going to happen, it will happen whether we worry about it or not, so why worry?

I remember the case of a woman and her daughter who came up to talk to me after I spoke at a meeting a few years ago. The woman was probably in her 50's and her daughter who lived with her was perhaps 30. They asked if I would come to their house as they had something very important and confidential they wanted to talk to me about. Also, I was told to come to the *back* door—not the front—a request which sounded rather strange.

A few days later when I went to their house, I discovered the reason. This woman and her daughter were living in a couple rooms at the back of their large old house. The front of the house was empty, the yard unkept. They did not want people to know that anyone was living there. The windows of the two rooms they lived in were covered with burlap. At nights only a dim light, if any was used. Why the would-be disguise? Why the strange and uncomfortable living conditions? These poor women imagined the *Communists* were after them; that the *Communists* were trying to *murder* them. Fear, especially in the mother, had become a mental obsession. "Fear hath *torment*" (1 John 4:18).

In his book *The Power of Positive Thinking*, Norman Vincent Peale has said that negative ideas should be eliminated from conversations. If you are with a group of people at a luncheon, for example, do not comment that the "Communists will soon take over the country", for in the first place, Communists are *not* going to take over the country and by saying things such as this, one only creates a depressing reaction in the minds of others.

ELECTION FEARS

Some people become fearful around election time. I heard a preacher say in 1960 that if Kennedy won the election, within six months he would have every Bible-believing church closed up! When Kennedy won the election, this man had a heart attack and almost died! I knew some lovely people who campaigned "for God and Goldwater." They believed that if Goldwater lost the election the tribulation would be upon us! Fear caused them to sell their home and property and move into a very remote area. Their lives would have been better, happier, and more productive if they had stayed right where they were. Too often people become alarmed about what this world leader or that is going to do. But we should remember that when Pilate said to Jesus: "Knowest thou not that I have power to crucify thee, and have power to release thee?", Jesus answered: "Thou couldest have no power at all against me, except it were given thee FROM ABOVE" (John 19:10, 11). I still believe it is God who makes and unmakes nations!

There are gloom and doom preachers who specialize in preaching *fear* more than faith. They suppose they must always tell the *bad* side of things. If they mention the president, it is only to criticize him. When they speak of America, it is almost always what is wrong—not what is *right*—with America. They talk about the problems, about how bad things are, about the short-comings, but seldom suggest practical answers. How can they? Their whole religious outlook is that everything will get worse and worse anyhow, nothing will turn out right.

With each new election or change (in this changing world), they suspect a vast conspiracy. They constantly live on the banks of Armageddon—and apparently feel they should preach fear all the time so they will have company. No wonder people don't want to go to church and hear long-winded sermons that are totally negative. I don't blame them! People have enough problems on the job, in the home, in the everyday activities of life. A church service ought to build them UP, not push them DOWN; should HELP, not HINDER them; should be based on FAITH, not FEAR!

I am not saying there are no problems or troubles in the world. But I think it is a question of where the *emphasis* should be placed. Paul said to think on things that are pure, lovely, and of *good report*. "And the PEACE of God, which passeth all under-standing, shall keep your hearts and minds through Christ Jesus" (Phil. 4:7, 8).

Fear is not of God. Why allow superstitious fears to rob and hinder your outlook on life? Why not commit your way unto the Lord? Jesus has promised us peace, even his peace, and tells us not to be afraid. "PEACE I leave with you, MY peace I give unto you...Let not your heart be troubled, neither let it be AFRAID" (John 14:27).

*   *   *   *   *

FIVE PRECIOUS THINGS

Things that are precious are things that are considered of great value, expensive, highly esteemed, dear. But, to me, the meaning seems to go deeper than this. If we refer to someone as a "precious person", we mean not only that he is a good person, a fine person, but that this person is especially dear to us, precious! The word "precious" is a precious word!

In the writings of Peter the apostle, there are five things which he mentioned as being precious: (1) precious trial, (2) precious blood, (3) precious savior, (4) precious faith, and (5) precious promises.

PRECIOUS TRIAL

"...the TRIAL of your faith, being much more PRECIOUS than of gold" (1 Peter 1:7). A precious trial? Normally we do not think of a trial as being precious! Are these not *strange* words coming from a man who knew what it was to be imprisoned, beaten, persecuted, and threatened for the cause of Christ? But Peter says: "Beloved, think it not *strange* concerning the fiery trial which is to try you...If any man suffer as a Christian...let him glorify God on this behalf" (1 Peter 4:12, 16).

The natural man who "receiveth not the things of the Spirit of God; for they are *foolishness* unto him" (1 Cor. 2:14) cannot comprehend such teaching. But when we realize that "all things work together for good to them that love God" (Rom. 8:28) and that "the steps of a good man are ordered by the Lord" (Psalms 37:23), we know that even trials must have a purpose. We are a part of a great, unfailing plan—God's plan!—and there are no accidents with Him who knows the end from the beginning! He has a way of turning trials into stepping stones to greater victories in Christ! Believing this, we can "give thanks always for *all things* unto God" and, as Peter said, "rejoice with joy unspeakable and full of glory"—even in the face of testing and trial (1 Peter 1:8).

We don't really understand victory without knowing defeat. We don't appreciate the mountain top until we have gone through the valley. We are thankful for the dawn because we have known a night. When flowers are crushed it brings forth their fragrance. So in life we too are crushed with trials at times—which have a purpose—and this purpose being accomplished we move on to the greater objectives of victorious living.

PRECIOUS BLOOD

"Ye were not redeemed with corruptible things, as silver and gold...but with the PRECIOUS BLOOD of Christ" (1 Peter 1:18, 19). Again, the natural man does not comprehend the great spiritual significance of the blood. Some churches object to preaching about the blood. They oppose blood songs in the hymn books. They cannot sing from their hearts: "There is power, power, wonder-working power in the blood of the Lamb!" or "Oh, *precious* is the flow that makes me white as snow!" They have not been able to figure out how garments can be washed in the blood of the Lamb and come out white! (Rev. 7:14).

But whether men like it or not, the Bible is a blood book—from Genesis to Revelation. In Genesis, the blood offering was respected (Gen. 4). In Exodus, God said: "When I see the blood, I will pass over you" (Exodus 12:13). In Leviticus we read: "For the life of the flesh is in the blood...it is the blood that maketh an atonement for the soul" (Lev. 17:11). And on through the Old Testament, we read of the sacrifices that were offered.

Then one day, right on schedule, Jesus appeared as the "Lamb of God" to take away the sins of the world by himself becoming the perfect sacrifice, shedding his blood in death, thus paying the penalty due to man for transgression. Since that time God has never accepted any other sacrifice for sins; nor will he ever do so in the future! As the book of Hebrews repeatedly points out, the sacrifice of Calvary was the eternal, the *final* sacrifice for sins forever!

In the book of Psalms we read: "As far as the east is from the west, so far hath he removed our transgressions from us" (Ps. 103:12). It does not say: "As far as the north is from the south", but "as far as the east is from the west."

If we go far enough south, we would pass the South Pole and be going north. If we go far enough north, we would pass the North

If we journeyed east, we would always be going east. Clearly there is no such thing as a place as far as the east is from the west! So far has God removed our sins through the redemption that is ours in Christ!

"Greater love hath no *man* than this, that a man lay down his life for his friends" (John 15:13). Man's love can be no greater than this. But the love of *God* is greater! Jesus not only gave his life for his FRIENDS, but even for his ENEMIES he died! "For scarcely for a righteous man will one die; yet peradventure for a good man some would dare to die. *But* God commendeth his love toward us, in that, while we were yet *sinners*, Christ died for us" (Rom. 5:7, 8). What love! This is the love of *God*! "For God *so loved* the world . . ." (John 3:16). Red or yellow, black or white, all are *precious* in his sight.

Peter, it should be noticed, makes it clear that redemption comes through the death of Christ, his shed blood—not by silver and gold! The price has already been paid. We are redeemed by the precious blood of Christ.

PRECIOUS SAVIOR

". . .unto you therefore which believe he is PRECIOUS" (1 Peter 2:3-7). To us who believe, he is more than a little baby in a manger. He is more than just a good man standing by the shore of Galilee. He is more than a lifeless savior hanging upon a cross. He is more than all of this, for he rose again from the dead, ascended into heaven, and is King of kings and Lord of lords (1 Tim. 6:15).

When he was born there was no room for him in the inn. But since that time millions have found room for him in their hearts and his presence has brought them peace and joy. He put on *humanity* that we might put on *divinity*. He became the son of *man* that we might become the sons of *God*. "He was in the world, and the world was made by him" (John 1:10). How strange that he who was *infinite* became a tiny *infant* —so small that a woman carried him around on the world he had created!

He was "despised and rejected of men" (Isaiah 53:3). Notice the following accusations that were made against him (and these I have taken just from the book of John!). They said he was a division maker (7:43), crazy (10:20), a blasphemer (10:33), illegitimate

(8:19), ungodly (9:16), a sinner (10:33), a deceiver (7:12), demon possessed (7:20), unpopular, unrecommended by religious leaders (7:48). "BUT as many as received him, to *them* gave he power to become the sons of God, even to them that believe on his name" (John 1:12)! As Peter said, "Unto you which believe he is *precious*"!

Herod could not kill him; people at a religious service could not stone him; Satan could not tempt him; death could not destroy him; the grave could not contain him! He is more wonderful and glorious than any artist could ever capture on canvas; all pictures of him fall far short of portraying the King in his beauty! We have a precious savior. No wonder the song writer said:

So *precious* is Jesus, my savior, my King,
His praise all the day long with rapture I sing;
To Him in my weakness for strength I can cling,
For He is so *precious* to me!

PRECIOUS FAITH

"Simon Peter, a servant and an apostle of Jesus Christ, to them that have obtained like PRECIOUS FAITH..." (2 Peter 1:11). At that time, the customary form for a letter was to put right at the beginning who the letter was *from* and who it was *to*. It was not a bad idea. Have you ever received a letter, wondered who it was from, and then had to look clear down at the end to see whose signature appeared? But at the time Peter wrote his epistle (letter), he followed the custom of clearing this matter up right at the start. Who was this letter from? Simon Peter. Who was it to? To them who had obtained like *precious* faith.

Right now I am reminded as I write of Psalm 133. "Behold, how *good* and how *pleasant* it is for brethren to dwell together in *unity*! It is like the *precious* ointment upon the head, that ran down upon Aaron's beard."

I like to have faith in people; I like people to have faith in me. When people lose faith in each other, discord results. When husband and wife lose faith in each other, homes are broken up. When nations lose faith in each other, wars result. But above and beyond all these forms of faith, we need "faith in God", for such faith knows no limitations. It laughs at impossibilities. Jesus said, "If you have faith...nothing shall be impossible to you" (Matt. 17:20). Unbelief may raise its ugly head and offer a thousand objections and excuses against such a positive concept, but true faith draws upon its own resources and always finds them sufficient.

Without *faith* it is impossible to please God. The just shall live by *faith*. The prayer of *faith* shall save the sick. Salvation itself is the gift of God through *faith*. *Faith* puts strength in Noah's arm to build an ark when there is no sign of a flood! *Faith* sends an army marching around Jericho's walls when "reason" suggests that it would take a million years to wear out those foundations by the tramp of marching feet! *Faith* pulls a nation to the edge of a deep and uncrossable ocean, only to find that its gates swing wide on the hinges of divine power and the paths of men are laid in the depths of the sea!

Let the storms of life come! Let the winds of adversity blow! Let disaster strike! If we have our faith, we have something precious—something that can carry us through and plant our feet on that solid rock that cannot be moved! Like Abraham who "staggered not at the promise of God...but was strong in faith, giving glory to God" (Rom. 4:20), we can rise up above our disappointments and discouragements and sing the song of triumph in the midst of seeming defeat...because of our *faith*! Indeed it is *precious*.

PRECIOUS PROMISES

"Whereby are given unto *us* exceeding great and PRECIOUS PROMISES: that by these ye might be partakers of the divine nature" (2 Peter 1:4). What are some of these precious promises? Here are some that have a strong meaning to me:

"I will never leave thee, nor forsake thee. So that we may boldly say, The Lord is my helper, and I will not fear what man shall do unto me" (Heb. 13:5, 6). "My help cometh from the Lord, which made heaven and earth" (Ps. 121:2). "I can do *all things* through Christ which strengtheneth me" (Phil. 4:13). "For it is *God* which worketh in you both to will and to do of his good pleasure" (Phil. 2:13).

"Greater is *he* that is in you, than he that is in the world" nature" (2 Peter 1:4). What are some of these precious promises? Here are some that have a strong meaning to me:

"I will never leave thee, nor forsake thee. So that we may boldly say, The Lord is my helper, and I will not fear what man shall do unto me" (Heb. 13:5, 6). "My help cometh from the Lord, which made heaven and earth" (Ps. 121:2). "I can do *all things* through Christ which strengtheneth me" (Phil. 4:13). "For it is *God* which worketh in you both to will and to do of his good pleasure" (Phil. 2:13).

"Greater is *he* that is in you, than he that is in the world" (1 John 4:4). "What shall we then say to these things? If God be for us, who can be against us? . . . In *all* these things we are *more than conquerors* through him that loved us" (Rom. 8:31, 37).

"Come unto me all ye that labor and are heavy laden, and I will give you *rest*" (Matt. 11:28). "And the *peace of God*, which passeth all understanding, shall keep your hearts and minds through Christ Jesus" (Phil. 4:7). "No good thing will he withhold from them that walk uprightly" (Psalms 84:11). "For the Lord is *good*" (Psalms 100:5). "God is *love*" (1 John 4:16). "In all thy ways acknowledge him, and *he* shall direct thy paths " (Proverbs 3:6).

"God is able to make *all* grace *abound* toward *you*; that ye, *always* having *all* sufficiency in *all things, may abound* to *every* good work" (2 Cor. 9:8). He is able to save to the uttermost (Heb. 7:25); able to keep that which we have committed unto him against that day (2 Tim. 1:12), "able to do *exceeding abundantly* above all that we ask or think according to the *power* that worketh is us" (Eph. 3:20). "Ye shall receive *power* after that the Holy Ghost is come upon you" (Acts 1:8). "The promise is unto you . . . to all that are afar off, even as many as the Lord our God shall call" (Acts 2:39). "For all the promises of God in him are yea, and in him amen, unto the glory of God" (2 Cor. 1:20).

*   *   *   *   *

"THERE IS A RIVER"

The story of the Bible begins and ends with a RIVER. In Genesis 2:10 we read: "And a RIVER went out of Eden to water the garden." In Revelation 22:1, 2 we read: "And he showed me a pure RIVER of life, clear as crystal, proceeding out of the throne of God."

What is a river? If we think about it, a river is water—a large amount of water. As such, a river is more than a brook or stream—a river has more water than these. Unlike a lake, the word "river" speaks of motion, of water moving, flowing. And in order to move or flow, a river continually receives more from a higher source. Thus a river is a perfect symbol for the blessings of God—blessings that are great, blessings that are abundant!

Within the river of divine blessings, God has promised *gladness*. "There is a RIVER, the streams whereof shall make *glad* the city of God" (Psalm 46:4). The context speaks of trouble, of the mountains being cast into the sea, and turmoil in the land. But even in the midst of adversity, though trouble may be on every hand, we may drink from the river of God and be glad.

Again, using the symbol of a river, God has promised spiritual *pleasures*—pleasures in abundance. "They shall be abundantly satisfied with the fatness of thy house; and thou shalt make them drink of the RIVER of thy *pleasures*" (Psalms 36:8). The word "pleasures" may, at first, cause some to think of pleasures in a worldly sense. The Bible does not deny there are pleasures in the world. The Bible tells us that Moses chose "rather to suffer affliction with the people of God, than to enjoy the pleasures of sin for a season" (Heb. 11:25). Here is the key. The pleasures of sin are only for a *season*, but the pleasures of God—which the world cannot give and cannot take away—are *eternal*! Not just for a season, or even for a lifetime, but "in thy presence is fulness of joy; at thy right hand there are pleasures for *evermore*" (Psalms 16:11).

There must have been a great joy in the heart of the prophet as he cried: "Look upon Zion . . . There the glorious Lord will be unto us a place of broad RIVERS and streams; wherein shall go no galley with oars, neither shall gallant ship pass thereby . . . and the inhabitant shall not say, I am sick: the people that dwell therein shall be forgiven their iniquity" (Isaiah 33:21-24). The river here described is not the kind on which a boat or ship would sail. It is spiritual. Such symbolism speaks of the blessings of God—of healing, of forgiveness, of mercy!

PEACE LIKE A RIVER

There is a little chorus called "I've Got Peace Like a River." A number of years ago I wondered if this was scriptural. Sometimes a river is not peaceful, I reasoned. Sometimes a river may overflow its banks during times of storm bringing death and destruction. But then I saw that the song was scriptural, for in Isaiah 66:12 we read: "I will extend peace to her like a RIVER." In what sense, then, does God give peace like a river? Certainly not in every sense of the word, for sometimes a river is not peaceful, but in the sense that a river can well symbolize *abundance*—continually receiving more from a higher source.

Imagine, for example, a man going down to the banks of the Mississippi river and trying to drink it dry! He could never exhaust such a supply. Even so, when we come to God, his provisions are abundant, more than sufficient. His peace flows in an inexhaustible supply!

EZEKIEL'S RIVER

In vision, Ezekiel was brought to "waters" that flowed from the house of God into the desert (Ezekiel 47). At first he was brought through the waters and "the waters were to the ankles." Later "the waters were to the knees." Still later "the waters were to the loins" and finally, the prophet declares that "it was a RIVER that I could not pass over: for the waters were risen, waters to swim in, a RIVER that could not be passed over."

Now without attempting a critical exposition of this passage, I simply want to draw a comparison. Some people start out in the Christian walk—they wade into the river of God until it is up to their ankles—and they stop. They have anklebone religion. Then there are others who are not content to merely stand by the shoreline. They do not want to remain "babes in Christ", but desire to grow. They wade out a little further—they get up to their knees. God blesses them. They suppose they have everything God has for them—and go no further!

Others venture on—into waters waist deep. They accept certain truths and, having received from the Lord, advance no further! But why not launch out into the deep—out where there are rivers of water to *swim* in? Why be content with anklebone religion, or kneebone religion, or merely wading in until the waters are waist deep? Surely God has more!

As long as Christ is uppermost and the scriptures are our guide, we will not go astray. Some are so afraid they might receive a false experience, they receive none at all. Such fear hinders faith, and according to our faith it will be done unto us. Jesus said if a child asks for bread, the father will not give him a stone. "How much more shall your heavenly Father give the Holy Spirit to them that ask him?" (Luke 11:11-13).

Someone says: "Do you believe in the 'second blessing'?" Yes, I do. I believe in the second, the third, the fourth, the fifth, the sixth—and a thousand blessings for that matter. But when people begin to think they have *everything* God has for them or they think they understand *everything* in the Bible, how can they receive more?

How often I have received letters from well-meaning individuals who are so wrapped up in one or two doctrinal points that they never move out into the river of God. There they are, standing ankle deep in the water, giving others the impression that their whole mission in life is to argue about one or two pet doctrines—especially points on which they *differ* with others! How many times have men formed religious denominations around a set of doctrines or rules, only to find that God's truth is marching on. This is why I do not believe in a closed creed. If I grow in grace and knowledge of Christ, certainly I should know more truth now than I did a year ago.

RIVERS IN THE DESERT

The river of Ezekiel's vision flowed forth into the desert and where it flowed it brought *life*. The prophet Isaiah spoke of "RIVERS of water in a dry place as the shadow of a great rock in a weary land" (Isaiah 32:2) and of "RIVERS in the desert" (Isaiah 43:19). Rivers of water in the *desert* are especially significant.

On numerous occasions I have traveled on highway 395 which is a route that runs north and south in the eastern part of California. For many miles, to the west of this desert highway are the mighty Sierra-Nevada mountains—very steep and rugged on this side. Among these peaks of solid rock is Mount Whitney (14,495 feet in elevation, highest point in the United States outside of Alaska) and not too far distant eastward in Death Valley is the lowest spot in the United States—282 feet below sea level.

Traveling this highway between these two extremes, it is a barren desert, unbroken except for an occasional stretch of trees extending from a mountain canyon. Immediately the trees reveal the presence of water. Sometimes there is sufficient water for the stream to come on down and cross beneath the road. It is a pleasant experience to stop by such streams in the desert. Waters in the desert are most impressive because of the *contrast*.

Perhaps you, dear reader, are going through a "dry place" in your spiritual experience. Right now, as you read these words, there may be problems you cannot seem to solve, questions that do not seem to have an answer, prayers that have gone unanswered. Perhaps you are in need of spiritual help, or you need a healing touch from the Lord, or you need a financial blessing. Just remember that our God has promised to be as rivers in the desert. Let your faith be inspired by this glad truth: it is in the "dry place" that the Lord has promised to be unto you as rivers of water! In this river of God there is a solution to your every need—spiritually, physically, financially. God's power has not been exhausted on some former generation, but flows today to meet your need.

Even great prophets of God had their tests, their "dry places". Yes, even prophets as famous as Elijah! We all know how he prayed and it did not rain on the land for three years and a half. We know of his victory against the prophets of Baal when he demonstrated that the God who answers by fire was indeed God. Surely the Lord was with Elijah. Yet, in the next scene, we see him so discouraged and afraid of Jezebel that he laid down under a juniper tree and wanted to die! But God was just as real—whether Elijah felt like it or not!

If we ever get discouraged, we can remember that so did Elijah—"a man subject to like passions as we are" (James 5:17). Our feelings of discouragement are no reason to give up. Though the clouds may for awhile obscure the sun, somewhere the sun is always shining. God is just as real as he ever was. Take courage, child of God, for without valleys there would be no mountain tops. Even though right now you may be in a desert place, so to speak, just remember that God has promised rivers in the desert! You are now in the place where you can experience the provisions of God and he can lead you into "green pastures."

RIVERS OF LIVING WATER

"In the *last* day, that *great* day of the feast, Jesus stood and cried, saying, If any man thirst, let him come unto me, and drink. He that believeth on me, as the scripture hath said, out of his belly shall flow rivers of living water" (John 7:37, 38). We notice that when Jesus spoke of this living water it was the last day, the great day of the feast which the Jews commemorated. These words become especially significant in view of the fact that on this very day a ritual which involved *water* was carried out.

While priests chanted the words of Isaiah 12:3, "Therefore with joy shall ye draw water out of the wells of salvation", a golden pitcher with water from the pool of Siloam was carried in solemn procession to the altar of sacrifice and its contents poured out. The ritual commemorated the time their forefathers had supernaturally received water from the smitten rock in the days of Moses. But for the majority of those people, what had been a reality in the days of Moses was now a thing of the past. Their religion had degenerated into mere ritualism. They talked of living water, their ceremonies symbolized it, they sang about it, but they failed to recognize in Jesus the very fountain of living waters.

It was in this setting—when the people were thinking of water—that Jesus spoke of the living water. The earthly waters of the ritual did not satisfy; the people were thirsty still. But through Jesus, we can find the true water, a satisfaction for our thirst, "a well of water springing up into everlasting life" (John 4:14)!

I say unto you: Are you thirsty? "Ho, everyone that thirsteth, come ye to the waters, and he that hath no money; come ye, buy, and eat; yea, come, buy wine and milk without money and without price" (Isaiah 55:1). "And the Spirit and the bride say, Come. And let him that heareth say, Come. And whosoever will, let him take the water of life freely" (Revelation 22:7).

OTHER
BOOKS BY RALPH WOODROW

BABYLON MYSTERY RELIGION

A complete Biblical and historical account of how ancient paganism was mixed with Christianity, especially at Rome. Complete. Footnotes, Ninety illustrations. $3.00.

GREAT PROPHECIES OF THE BIBLE

Will the return of Christ be in two stages? The historicist view concerning the abomination of desolation, tribulation, Jacob's trouble, the 70th week of Daniel, the Anti-Christ. $3.00

HIS TRUTH IS MARCHING ON!

Advanced studies on prophecy in the light of history. Ezekiel 38, the coming of Elijah, Zechariah 14—future or fulfilled? The kingdom of God—present or postponed? Do the scriptures teach a Jewish-type millennium? $3.00

Prices include postage.

ORDER FROM:
Ralph Woodrow
P. O. Box 124
Riverside, California 92502